On Liberty

SHAMI CHAKRABARTI

On Liberty

ALLEN LANE
an imprint of
PENGUIN BOOKS

ALLEN LANE

Published by the Penguin Group
Penguin Books Ltd, 80 Strand, London WC2R ORL, England
Penguin Group (USA) Inc., 375 Hudson Street, New York, New York 10014, USA
Penguin Group (Canada), 90 Eglinton Avenue East, Suite 700, Toronto, Ontario, Canada M4P 2Y3
(a division of Pearson Canada Inc.)
Penguin Ireland, 25 St Stephen's Green, Dublin 2, Ireland (a division of Penguin Books Ltd)
Penguin Group (Australia), 707 Collins Street, Melbourne, Victoria 3008, Australia
(a division of Pearson Australia Group Pty Ltd)
Penguin Books India Pvt Ltd, 11 Community Centre, Panchsheel Park, New Delhi – 110 017, India
Penguin Group (NZ), 67 Apollo Drive, Rosedale, Auckland 0632, New Zealand
(a division of Pearson New Zealand Ltd)
Penguin Books (South Africa) (Pty) Ltd, Block D, Rosebank Office Park,
181 Jan Smuts Avenue, Parktown North, Gauteng 2193, South Africa

Penguin Books Ltd, Registered Offices: 80 Strand, London WC2R ORL, England

www.penguin.com

First published 2014
006

Copyright © Shami Chakrabarti, 2014

The moral right of the author has been asserted

Lines from 'Big Yellow Taxi' by Joni Mitchell reproduced by kind permission of Alfred Music.

Every effort has been made to contact copyright holders.
The author and publishers would be glad to amend in future editions
any errors or omissions brought to their attention.

Set in 10.75/14 pt Sabon LT Std
Typeset by Jouve (UK), Milton Keynes
Printed in Great Britain by Clays Ltd, St Ives plc

ISBN: 978-1-846-14809-5

www.greenpenguin.co.uk

MIX
Paper from
responsible sources
FSC
www.fsc.org FSC® C018179

Penguin Books is committed to a sustainable
future for our business, our readers and our planet.
This book is made from Forest Stewardship
Council™ certified paper.

For my son the Bean

Contents

Introduction

This book has been a dozen years or perhaps a lifetime or several in the making. It is my story and the story of Liberty (the National Council for Civil Liberties, NCCL) in the difficult and soul-defining decade or so leading up to its eightieth birthday. It is also more than this. *On Liberty* is an attempt to explain both the values and some of the important struggles of so many people who believe in the precious treasure of fundamental rights and freedoms that binds people and democratic societies together. From 9/11 to unprecedented state surveillance and attacks on the Human Rights Act; my leap from the Home Office, to the birth of my son and death of my mother. This is an account of my personal and political journey.

These are challenging times for human rights. The ill-judged and misnamed 'War on Terror' has morphed into a permanent state of exception becoming the rule. This has been triggered not only by horrific crimes against people and the terror of collapsing towers but by collapsing markets, economies and institutions. No one is above the law. Yet some have readily decided that the rule of law is too exacting and human rights principles too expensive in times of insecurity and austerity.

As I write, some senior figures in the Conservative Party and the UK Independence Party that has so tweaked its tail propose abolishing the Human Rights Act and withdrawing from the European Convention on Human Rights. They are wrong. This is written as much for you (if you prove open or curious enough to dip into it) as for any of us. Our responsibility is to previous generations who fought for rights and freedoms and to future ones, for whom we hold them in trust.

At Liberty House in Westminster, I have the privilege of working with the kindest, cleverest and most creative young professionals. We always say that reading sympathetic newspapers while listening to chattering radio and sipping a fair-trade organic brew is all very well in the kitchen on your own time, but campaigning it is not. Human rights sceptics and critics have had undue influence over the last few years – and that has been reflected in the media and in government policy and rhetoric. It is exactly these naysayers that we must persuade that far from being trivial luxuries to be sacrificed in times of strife, our small bundle of non-negotiable freedoms upheld by the rule of law is essential to everything that makes our lives worth living – from protection against torture and the right to a fair trial and private life to freedoms of conscience, speech and association. Lawyers can number, translate and contest the application of our rights to particular circumstances. But these values can be summed up by three little words: dignity, equality and fairness. These are the ideas from which our various human rights flow and for reasons this book explains, the greatest of these is equality.

Liberty was formed in 1934 in an ostensibly very different world. There was no internet, CCTV or DNA profiling. However, everyone had recent experience of the horrors of war. Many endured genuine economic hardship. The far right was gaining ground and national newspapers regularly voiced their disgust at the arrival of refugees from Eastern Europe. But the particular jolt for Liberty's founders was seeing hunger marchers from the North of the country meeting an especially brutal reception at the hands of the Metropolitan Police in London's Hyde Park in November 1932. The marchers brought a petition a million signatures strong and protested against a 10 per cent cut in unemployment benefit and the means test imposed the previous year. What's more, they had been infiltrated by undercover police acting as *agents provocateurs*, inciting demonstrators to violence so as to justify a violent police response. In the intervening years some things have changed for the better and some not nearly enough.

Our founders formed the National Council for Civil Liberties 'to keep watch over the entire spirit of British liberty'. Today they might have blogged and tweeted this resolve. After their inaugural meeting on 24 February 1934 in the crypt of St Martin-in-the-Fields in Trafalgar Square, they announced their new organization in a letter to the *Manchester Guardian*. The signatories included Clement Attlee, Vera Brittain, H. G. Wells, Edith Summerskill MP and the first Secretary of the NCCL, Ronald Kidd. Kidd was a civil servant, journalist, publisher and even actor before finding his place in the world as a civil liberties campaigner. He and a small group of brave people of values and ideals set in motion a campaign which would become the oldest human rights group in the UK.

After the Second World War freedom struggles around the world found international solidarity and intellectual cohesion within the framework of the 1948 Universal Declaration of Human Rights. The UDHR is a global expression of rights to which all humans are inherently entitled. Regional and local documents followed, including Churchill's legacy, the European Convention on Human Rights. This is an essential text that I came to know as a law student in the early 1990s when human rights were an almost exotic international study option. I applied it later as a government lawyer in the Home Office while advising on and defending decisions, policy and legislation in the European Court of Human Rights (ECtHR). You might say that I am a Jedi Knight who began on the dark side of the force.

In 1998, a young New Labour government took a bill through Parliament with significant cross-party support incorporating most of the Convention articles into UK law. Now they could be enforced in local courts with a greater understanding of domestic culture and context and without claimants having to make the sometimes decade-long hike to Strasbourg. This was an incredibly important moment for the UK. The Human Rights Act provided our modern Bill of Rights. It is this short but essential list of protections for the vulnerable against the powerful, the individual against the state and their availability to people in the United Kingdom that has become so controversial in recent years.

My work at Liberty has been second only to motherhood as the joy and privilege of my life. Yet just as I never expected to find work that would be quite so rewarding, I never expected to have to make arguments against internment, kidnap and torture in freedom's name, or for the retention and defence of universal human rights in principle in one of the oldest unbroken democracies on earth.

For just as a belief in fundamental rights and freedoms is common in all areas of mainstream democratic politics, so it seems these days is their denial. Over the years I have talked to many highly educated and senior UK politicians who espouse a belief that an independent or 'unelected' judiciary is somehow 'undemocratic' and that the only legitimate power is their own. These increasingly shrill voices lack both intellectual humility and constitutional literacy or understanding of the foundations upon which our democracy rests. To elect judges is like nominating a referee from one or other football team. It would ensure that in times of strife and even more routinely, the roar of the crowd rules and Barabbas goes free. I sometimes wonder whether this new, arrogant and increasingly detached political class has thought at all deeply about what democracy means and what it needs to survive.

By analogy, many of us are lectured daily about the virtues of unfettered markets; not just as the best means of providing material benefits to the greatest number, but as a kind of evolutionary natural selection which must be unencumbered by rules and regulation. But even the most bloodless free-marketeer generally understands the essential nature of having 'rules of the game'. At the very least, there must be effective criminal law to prevent people from robbing each other, civil law to bind them to the bargains which they have struck with one another and probably a great deal of complex company, competition and other regulatory law besides. Without these laws today's market eats itself and descends into tomorrow's monopoly, oligarchy or gangster paradise.

Democracy also needs rules. Imagine a charismatic leader sweeps to victory with a massive majority in, for example, a parliamentary system such as the United Kingdom. She now wields massive power and influence in both executive and legislative branches of state and in the media as well. Once the electoral honeymoon is over, critical news coverage of and comment on the new government's policies begin to irritate our heroic premier. She decides that such interventions are nothing short of sedition and worthy of censure and prosecution. Soon political opponents are arrested on tenuous grounds by ever more politicized law enforcers, and judges are threatened and attacked for doing their job of holding the government accountable under the law. The government decides that the administration costs of the next general election are prohibitively expensive in the worst recession in living memory and so it should be deferred until the economy is on a more even keel. A fanciful scenario? Perhaps, but one that I have seen in my lifetime elsewhere in the world. Rules in the form of human rights and the rule of law prevent majority rule descending into that of the mob and today's democracy from becoming tomorrow's dictatorship.

One question that people put to me up and down the country time and again is: 'Isn't there too much talk about rights and not enough about responsibilities?' As I have chosen social responsibility as a way of life, this can be an emotionally tough question. However, if I stop to think about it for a minute, it is far less tricky intellectually. The modern world is highly regulated by a multitude of obligations. Criminal law and civil and administrative duties govern every aspect of our lives. So it hardly seems excessive that our elected representatives who govern us owe us a small bag of duties as well. This means respecting our freedoms and accepting a few obligations to create a society and infrastructure in which we are protected from each other. This is a positive responsibility on the state to protect the rights and freedoms of the people and not merely a negative restraint. It requires effective criminal law and its enforcement, effective access to justice and the protection of the individual from overweening bureaucracy and the vulnerable from the physically and materially powerful in society.

What are these fundamental rights, rules and values that some find so difficult to stomach? What are the freedoms too often described as alien, unworkable or old-fashioned? This so-called 'criminals' charter' protects all of us. It provides our right to life and not to be tortured, enslaved or thrown into arbitrary detention. It guarantees the right to a fair trial and respect for our private and family lives. Freedoms of conscience, speech and association are enshrined and, most importantly of all, equal treatment under the law for everyone, no matter how rich or poor, privileged or disenfranchised. These concepts reflect the idea that as human beings we are precious individuals and inherently social creatures rubbing along together in democratic society – a term referred to often in the Convention. These ideas are neither selfish individualism nor the 'political correctness' that some label them, seeking to diminish their worth. Rather they provide safeguards for every civil and political sphere of our lives, from the intimate area of private thoughts and family life through to speech, expression and association with others. This includes friendly, faith-based, family, trade union, neighbourhood and political relationships and all the bonds that make our society.

The late great Lord Tom Bingham, perhaps the finest judge of recent times, asked:

Which of these rights, I ask, would we wish to discard? Are any of them trivial, superfluous, unnecessary? Are any of them un-British? There may be those who would like to live in a country where these rights are not protected, but I am not of their number.

Nor am I. Tom said this in his address to Liberty's 75th Anniversary Conference in 2009, as he emphasized the need to defend the Human Rights Act (HRA), as our modern bill of rights protecting both parliamentary sovereignty and the rule of law. Not all of its friends and even fewer of its critics have actually read the seminal piece of 1998 legislation. Drafted by Sir Edward Caldwell CB QC, former First Parliamentary Counsel, it is one of the most simply and elegantly crafted Acts of Parliament of our lifetime.

The rights and freedoms I mention above are listed in the Act and protected by this piece of special legislation. It is vital to remember that nearly all of them (the most obvious exceptions being protections from torture and slavery) need to be balanced against the rights and freedoms of other people. They can be proportionately interfered with if necessary for certain good reasons, such as public health and order, the prevention and detection of crime and national security. This seems most evidently true of privacy, conscience, association and even free speech and expression. Speech is often described as an absolute right in other parts of the world but it can never be absolute in practice.

So much inevitable balancing in the practical application of these fundamental rights and freedoms makes aspects of the HRA and Convention especially important. Firstly, the HRA rightly allows the courts to strike down the unlawful acts and decisions of local and central government administrations and ministers. This is something they were able to do under UK law long before the Act was passed. While it requires that legislation be read compatibly with human rights whenever that is possible, Parliament (as opposed to the government) retains the final word, even over the judiciary. Therefore rules and regulations over which government has near complete control and which are passed with very little parliamentary scrutiny may be struck down if contrary to human rights. But if the words of an Act of Parliament are too clearly incompatible with human rights, the senior judges may only make what the Human Rights Act describes as a 'declaration of incompatibility'. This says that the Act of Parliament cannot possibly be reconciled with human rights. This is very powerful. It has moral, political and persuasive effect in any democracy that respects the rule of law. Despite this moral force, the bad legislation stays in place unless Parliament chooses to change it.

This seems to me to be a typical British constitutional compromise. It asserts human rights in the courtroom and parliamentary chamber, while recognizing that the sovereignty of Parliament remains the overarching principle of our system in the UK. The HRA also requires our courts to 'take account of' the decisions of the Strasbourg Human Rights Court rather than be bound by them. Contrary to the ignorant ranting of many a human rights sceptic, it expressly preserves our national as well as parliamentary sovereignty. I have been alarmed that this has not prevented successive Home Secretaries complaining about interfering 'unelected judges' impeding some of their decisions, especially in relation to deportation. However *parliamentary* sovereignty is not the same as the supremacy of the *executive*. Nor do we want it to be in any democratic system where the law binds and protects everyone alike and operates as a vital check on abuses of power.

In my experience, whatever our instinctive groans and grumbles from time to time, we all believe in human rights when we are considering our own rights, and those of people we love or 'people like us'. It is when these rights apply to 'others' that there are problems. You might say that my speech is free and yours just that little bit more expensive. The principle of equal treatment under the law provides the solution. As Rabinder Singh QC (now Singh J) wrote, equal treatment imposes a legal discipline on democratic majorities who might otherwise make compromises and trade-offs in relation to the freedoms of disenfranchised minorities that the more powerful group would never tolerate for itself. Think of how asylum seekers and schoolchildren have been subjected to routine fingerprinting and how foreign nationals are always politically the easiest to detain without charge or trial. In these cases, the principle of equal treatment forces courtrooms and ballot boxes to work together to protect the rights and freedoms of everyone. Legal language calls it 'non-discrimination'; we all know it as empathy.

The idea of walking in another's shoes and doing to others as we would have done to us is universal in all cultures of the world. It does not require a blind disregard for the greater good, but it does mean that no one should be completely excluded or thrown away. It also demands from us a modicum of respect for other people, even for those who have lost respect for others and themselves. It cannot be limited or rationed according to nationality. Replacing the Human Rights Act and Convention with a British bill of rights is an attempt to redefine our fundamental rights as citizens' privileges. This is nothing short of the road to Guantanamo Bay, where it has been regarded acceptable for US administrations to intern and mistreat foreign nationals offshore.

The world is shrinking and ever more interconnected. We have to decide whether to seek protection as human beings everywhere or live with the vulnerability of being foreigners in every country other than our own. I know which state of being I choose and in which direction I want my country to lead.

I

2001: 'Nothing to Hide, Nothing to Fear': the Fishbowl and the Three-walled Prison

If you give me six lines written by the hand of the most honest of men, I will find something in them which will hang him.

— Cardinal Richelieu*

I am sure that everyone over the age of thirty remembers where they were on Tuesday 11 September 2001. I had left the Home Office not long after the 2001 general election for a newly created job as in-house counsel at Liberty. My last brief as a lawyer in the department included anti-terror work and some, but by no means all, my senior colleagues had thought the intended move disloyal. So I was referred to the Cabinet Office. Government rightly has rules to ensure that those responsible for dishing out large-scale defence contracts do not move too easily to the private companies they have rewarded. As a public lawyer, I had no such responsibility or incentive, but given Liberty's obvious interest in the type of work I had been doing, I didn't just give notice but asked for permission to take up the new post. After a few difficult months my departure was cleared by a committee chaired by the well-respected former Conservative Attorney General, the late Lord Mayhew. I was released on

* Quoted in *Cyclopaedia of Practical Quotations* (1896) by Jehiel Keeler Hoyt, p. 763

the understanding that I remain a barrister and bound in confidentiality to any former client, including the government.

I went from the plush offices of a well-kept government building to the tatty converted shop that was then Liberty's base. I spent my first day absorbing the culture shock of my move from a Goliath department of state to a David-size NGO. There was warmth and good intention but little focus or natural light. It was days before anyone would fix my computer, but in contrast with the rather bizarre practice in much of the public sector, the employer provided milk for tea and coffee. I remember looking in the fridge and asking about the ownership of a particular carton. A bemused new colleague gave the wonderful reply: 'That's Liberty milk.' I was told that I had been employed to inject strategic thinking into Liberty litigation and went home musing on the likely challenges and priorities for the next few years.

My second day at work was 11 September. After lunch with one of my new colleagues I returned to the news of a plane crashing into the first tower of the World Trade Center. Young trainees and interns followed events on their computers rather than TV – a new phenomenon. Was it a hideous accident? But that sick feeling in the stomach was quickly answered by the images of the second plane.

What a moment to have left the security business in pursuit of civil liberties. I sat at my new desk facing the wall. I couldn't reach my old schoolfriend in Manhattan on the phone. Where and how were other loved ones? I worried for my friends and colleagues back in the Dark Tower, as I affectionately thought of the Home Office, which I imagined to be another target.

So I can hardly underestimate the shock to the American psyche caused by the images and reality of civil aeroplanes converted into deadly missiles attacking downtown Manhattan in a hideous 'spectacular' so obviously designed to create a feeling of vulnerability and panic in what at the time was probably accurately describable as the world's only superpower. Perhaps only the surprise bombing of the US Hawaiian naval base at Pearl Harbor sixty years earlier could even vaguely compare. Elsewhere in the world, including in my own home city of London, people had from time to time become all too used to, even stoic about, terrorist attacks, whose impact then diminished somewhat.

Yet, as hours, days and weeks passed and the initial shock and reflection gave way to hawkish opportunism in Washington and London, my own momentary pessimism grew into a more positive resolve. Perhaps I was in the right place after all. Now more than ever, I found value in values that cherish both safety and liberty. And it would prove useful to have some understanding and experience of a political system that we respect but still must hold to account. I certainly began to see the importance of Liberty and human rights when fear stalks the land.

Things were going to change – that much was obvious. I watched three trends very quickly emerging from the political and legislative response to the horror of 9/11. The death of privacy, the denigration of due process (access to fair legal trials) and the deliberate and determined discrimination against 'others', Muslims and foreign nationals in particular, with especially harsh treatment that won't do for the majority population – at least at first. All three represent a kind of attack on 'the presumption of innocence', if as I do, you see it as a way of looking at people and the world and not merely a rule for the courtroom.

Tony Blair famously and perhaps commendably dashed to the United States in solidarity with its people and President at the first news of the Twin Towers atrocity. Sadly this friendship did not translate into passing on the wisdom of past failed British anti-terror internment policies but instead into emulating the younger nation's new error. Two years later Richard Curtis's romantic comedy *Love Actually* would depict a youngish charismatic British prime minister (played by Hugh Grant) standing up to the bullying behaviour and policies of the American president (played by Billy Bob Thornton):

We may be a small country, but we are a great one. A country of
Shakespeare, Churchill, the Beatles, Sean Connery, Harry Potter,
David Beckham's right foot, David Beckham's left foot come to
that . . .

Whether you find the speech stirring or schmalzy, it could
well have done with Magna Carta added to its list. Sadly, the
success of this particular popular movie moment was obviously
aspirational rather than historical. Unlike the romantic hero of
the film, Mr Blair appeared to adopt the thinking of his coun-
terpart, even down to the targeting of foreign nationals in an
attempt to circumvent the normal and ancient rigours of fair
trial rights under the criminal law.

The death of privacy has affected everyone, if only subtly
and incrementally. Stories about giant government databases
and the creeping prevalence of CCTV have led to a casualness,
a presumption that of course you are being watched, of course
'they' are listening in. Do you know the fable of 'the frog-broiler
experiment'? It was told to me some time later by the then government chief scientist Professor Sir David King, but you can read
a thousand versions on the internet. The theory is that a frog
placed in a pan of boiling water will instantly (instinctively,
intelligently or both) jump out and save his skin. On the other
hand, if the frog is sitting happily in a pan of room-temperature
or tepid water and heat is gently and gradually applied, our
amphibious friend will splash around oblivious as he slowly boils
to death. This metaphor works well for complacency towards
our civil liberties in general, but best encapsulates the easy
death of privacy.

After 9/11 senior politicians quickly rushed to the micro-
phones with the unexamined blanket edict that everyone would
have to get used to less personal privacy. The new Foreign Secretary and previous occupant of the Dark Tower told the BBC
Radio 4 *Today* programme on 28 September 2001:

It wasn't Big Brother government. It was government trying to put in place increased powers so we could preserve our democracy against this new type of threat. Now people are saying: 'Why are these terrorists here?'

A simple exchange was asserted and offered: less general liberty, especially privacy, in return for greater security. And even if you could – who would refuse? After all, it's not like subjecting millions of people to more acute human rights violations such as incarceration or torture.

In frightening times especially, protecting your privacy can feel a bit of a bourgeois luxury, like net curtains or a garden hedge. Time and again the trade-off seems at first so attractive. A little identity card that links your personal information to a big computer. A painless saliva swab and retained DNA of everyone arrested whether ever charged with, let alone convicted of, a crime. Cameras everywhere and later, as people came to live more and more of their lives online, 'the Snoopers' Charter' to license the blanket retention and monitoring of everyone's complete web-life: every email, skype session, visit to a website. What's the problem, you paranoid libertarian loon? The innocent surely have nothing to fear?

But we all have something to hide or at least to protect. We all have a wealth of past, permanent or potential information about us that could in the right or wrong hands lead to abuse by accident or design. And the appetite for data collection is rarely easily sated. When identity cards were introduced in Britain during the Second World War they carried just a few pieces of identifying information about the holder. By the time the scheme was eventually abandoned years later after complaints from disgruntled citizens tired of having to produce the document for no good reason, the amount of personal information held on the card had multiplied several times. And this even without the aid of computer databases.

The way in which we enjoy and understand privacy can be highly culturally sensitive. European cousins who express horror at London as the CCTV capital of the world shrug their shoulders at our resistance to carrying identity cards. Conversely, even President Bush, even after 9/11, found identity cards too authoritarian a step for the American people. So what was the problem with ID cards? My concerns were always threefold.

Firstly, we live in a country without a written constitution, entrenched bill of rights or even strong law of privacy. What has somehow compensated for centuries, is a libertarian instinct that demands that the police officer should identify himself to us and we need do likewise only with reasonable cause.

Secondly, as proposed in the Queen's Speech in November 2003, the National Identity Register – the gargantuan centralized database to which ID cards would be linked – was going to provide a system like none before. It would have a huge capacity to hold reams of private information centrally, providing a honeypot for fraudsters and terrorists alike. It was intended to hold at least fifty pieces of information on every adult who had been in the UK for more than three months. This vast amount of data would have been an enormous vulnerability – all that information about you, held in one place, ripe for identity theft. Crucially, unlike traditional identity cards, where both the subject and the authorities can look at the same information in plain view and contest its veracity, the proposed system would leave the holder in the dark as to just how much information and of what accuracy was being collected, held and interpreted by those with power over him. This creates a huge distinction with identity documents for specific purposes, such as passports, bank or national insurance cards and even the databases which sit behind them. In these cases, the database should, by definition, hold only such information as is relevant to the obvious and stated aim of the enterprise (proof of nationality, banking facility or right to work).

In the years of the British political battles over ID cards, they were at times, it seemed, offered up as a panacea for everything except global warming. Ministers told us that terrorism would be prevented. And yet we know suicide bombers are more than happy to be identified. Benefit fraud would be foiled – even though most of it relates to alleged health or circumstances rather than identity. And of course the flow of illegal immigration would be stemmed once and for all.

And in this third point lies the rub. For if identity cards are to be used to deal with illegal immigration, a country is moving from immigration control purely or predominantly at the border to 'in-country' control on the streets. Ask a French-Algerian or a German-Turk whether they feel as comfortable with the obligation to show papers on demand as their white neighbours and friends. Inevitably, if such control is a stated purpose and the authorities have the power to check the status of anyone on any street in their country, who do you think is going to be stopped umpteen times a day, week and year? The experience of police powers to stop and search without suspicion should persuade you of the dangers of granting indiscriminate power of this kind.

So as many to the centre-right of British politics reviled the Blair–Blunkett ID card ambitions from a libertarian 'rights of free-born Englishman' instinct, some to the left knew what a tool for racial oppression identity cards would be. Labour MP Diane Abbott once described them as 'a new pass law in our inner cities'. The Rt Hon. David Davis MP, long the champion for civil liberties on the right, dismissed them as 'a massive reversal of the relationship between the citizen and the state'. Davis and Abbott are both right and it has been a privilege to sometimes see such cross-spectrum coalescing around democratic values that are not always the most popular.

Our DNA isn't just an identifier like a fingerprint or signature. It can reveal extremely private things about our familial past and predicted future; things we don't know ourselves and might not want to know. Your true parentage for example, or a genetic condition which makes you uninsurable. In the criminal justice context DNA can obviously provide vital evidence of identity and location, capable of incriminating or exculpating a suspect. But think of the dangers of discrimination, blunder and abuse if the most intimate information of millions of innocents is stockpiled for ever, as though we're all suspects now. Later, at the height of the mass-retention policy in 2006, the compulsory garnering of everyone's DNA was mooted by then Prime Minister Tony Blair, but no draft legislation was ever brought before Parliament. Perhaps the image of millions of grandmothers, toddlers and everyone in between queuing up at the police station or GP's surgery to give a strand of hair or saliva swab under pain of prosecution for non-compliance was, in the end, thought too distasteful and unattractive to be achieved overnight.

Instead the database grew by stealth until Britain's was the largest in the world. The police were using their power to take the DNA of arrested people and then never destroyed it, even if they were let go moments later, were never charged or even were acquitted by the courts. Don't get me wrong, DNA must be an investigative as well as an evidential tool. I have no problem with taking the DNA of someone arrested on suspicion of a serious offence to which it might be relevant (such as a sex or violent crime or burglary). It could be highly indicative as to who littered the street with cigarette butts, but I consider that offence too trivial. Insider dealing can be very serious but it is hard to see how DNA might help solve or prove the crime. However, as we have a criminal justice system built on the presumption of innocence, we arrest on suspicion, charge with evidence and convict on proof. Of course the authorities should have a reasonable period to retain identifying information in case something else turns up, but this cannot last for ever.

While the 2001 legislation theoretically allowed officers discretion to destroy entries, ministerial exhortation and ACPO

(Association of Chief Police Officers) policy made such discretion a myth, unless challenged by the wealthy, lawyers or celebrity. Inevitably, as arrest – with the low threshold of 'reasonable suspicion' of criminality – was the trigger for taking a sample in the police station, a wholly disproportionate percentage of young black men in particular found themselves on the database permanently without ever having been convicted of a crime. My genetic privacy is free; theirs is a little more expensive. It eventually took a Strasbourg Court of continental judges (some no doubt with memories of less than democratic regimes) to rule against it in the case of *S & Marper v United Kingdom*. They may have imagined the potential horrors of 'blanket and indiscriminate' DNA retention. The obvious irony of 'indiscriminate' policy is that it invariably proves highly 'discriminatory' in practice.

The 'nothing to hide, nothing to fear' debate would rage well into the next decade, and well beyond the New Labour government. It has forced me to reflect a great deal on the individual and societal value of privacy. For it isn't just the obvious authoritarians who sometimes overlook it. When you spend your life hearing testimony of the gravest human rights abuses around the world, the imposition of even omnipresent surveillance can seem pretty tame by comparison. If you ever drift into feeling this way, try to see the wonderful 2006 German film *Das Leben der Anderen* (*The Lives of Others*), set in the old East Germany under the grip of the Stasi (secret police). It presents a moving but never sentimental or hysterical account of life without privacy with which I find it hard to compete and yet, for the sake of completeness, will try.

If all our fundamental rights flow from dignity, equality and fairness, respect for private and family life (Article 8 of the European Convention on Human Rights) is obviously inherent to dignity. In the introduction I argued that the legal protection of our civil and political rights is essential to the preservation of democracy itself. However, these rights are also a reflection and protection of what it is to be human. From a very early age we protect our modesty and privacy, closing the bathroom or bedroom door, or at least wishing to. This instinct appears universal in communities however rural or remote, the world over. Because we are social creatures who come together in families, communities and societies for all sorts of beneficial activity our privacy cannot be absolute. Yet without it altogether, how can there be any dignity, intimacy or trust? Further, it is hard to imagine how other vital freedoms can flourish in the fishbowl under the constant gaze of the state. How can you secure sound elections without a secret ballot or fair trials without confidential legal counsel? Where is the space for true freedom of conscience or association if personal reflection or meetings with others of our choosing cannot be in private? Even free speech, which is so often apparently in tension with personal privacy, is sometimes quite dependent upon it. Think of how jealously a journalist will guard her confidential sources or the greater courage that some find when writing anonymously (whether online or offline).

For our rights and freedoms are not like those pick-and-mixes that we knew in old-fashioned sweet shops and find again in the foyers of modern multiplex cinemas. You can't take free speech while dumping personal privacy. The values are as interdependent as the people they protect. In particular, when 'balanced' or 'qualified' rights like privacy are compromised too sloppily without rational and proportionate justification or defined limits, the inevitable outcome in practice is significant discrimination in the application of the intrusive power. So-called 'blanket' power is rarely truly universal in practice or effect. Look at the astonishing proportion of black men on the DNA database – almost 40 per cent – or who find themselves subject to stop and search without suspicion – on average six times as likely as white people.

But discrimination is not only casual, careless or inadvertent.

It can also come by the deliberate design of policy and legislation. Just as many people were subtly or slightly more intrusively affected by the US–UK domestic responses to the 9/11 atrocity, others were singled out for a more direct, determined and acute violation of rights. Guantanamo Bay was an almost fictional place which many of us had previously associated with either the jolly summer song 'Guantanamera' or the 1992 Rob Reiner–Aaron Sorkin courtroom drama *A Few Good Men*. Now, it stands as an icon of injustice: a prison camp and 'legal black hole', where 'enemy combatants' have been detained without charge and mistreated for well over a decade in freedom's name at the hands of one of the world's most mature democracies. How was it possible? How did clever constitutionally literate people advise and then sanction such an obviously counterproductive scandal; a festering sore on the conscience of the democratic world that would give succour to anti-Western anger everywhere?

The sight of passenger aircraft ploughing into two of the central pillars of the New York skyline at the cost of nearly 3,000 lives brought home the precariousness and vulnerability of life. It was shocking, sudden, cruel – and man-made. It surely says something about the fragility of 'constitutionalism' and any bill of rights based more on citizenship than humanity that lawyers felt able to advise President Bush that the combination of an offshore location and foreign nationality could make Guantanamo and its eventual inmates a non-place full of non-people for the purposes of the law.

As far as I know, there are no obvious musical or cinematic references to Belmarsh Prison or to Thamesmead in South London, where the ugly and bleak container sits. Belmarsh was the location for the United Kingdom's own experiment in twenty-first-century internment, which took place for over four years from the winter of 2001. Nothing as crude perhaps as orange jumpsuits and an exotic offshore venue for Her Majesty's government, but nonetheless, here too, the foreign nationality of terrorist suspects became justification for detention without charge or trial.

The creative device on this side of the Atlantic was not an offshore island but immigration law which had long and understandably allowed migrants to be detained for purposes of border control: for examination on entry and for the purposes of effecting removal or deportation of an unwelcome or overstayed visitor. Even so, this type of administrative detention by the UK Secretary of State is not incompatible with the right to personal liberty and the right against arbitrary detention under Article 5 of the Human Rights Convention, as long as it is necessary to the stated purpose, provided for in legislation and subject to scrutiny and appeals in the appropriate courts and tribunals.

Back in 1996, I had not long arrived in Mordor, yet another nickname for the Home Office. The UK government lost what was to become a seminal legal case in the Strasbourg Court of Human Rights. Mr Chahal was an Indian national who had been living in Britain since the early 1970s when he came to the attention of the authorities on suspicion of involvement with Sikh separatist-inspired terrorism. He was detained pending deportation to India where, he claimed, he would be subject to torture. By the 1990s, there was already a well-established system of tribunals to provide scrutiny of and appeals against immigration decisions, but in 'national security cases' (where the Home Secretary signed a certificate that a particular person was non-conducive to the public good on national security grounds) proper appeals were replaced by a paper review by retired judges (often referred to as 'three wise men') over lunch in the House of Lords.

Chahal ended up being detained for over six years without proper legal scrutiny. Unsurprisingly, the European Court of Human Rights was not amused and in 1996 established some important principles which have had a significant impact on

subsequent UK security policy. One principle was that to satisfy Article 5, the right to liberty, there must be some kind of
proper legal scrutiny and redress, even in national security
cases. Another crucial principle is that the absolute rule against
torture and inhuman and degrading treatment under Article
3 does not refer only to torture by the direct hands of agents of
a signatory state. That state will also be responsible if it sends
someone under its control to a place of torture elsewhere. This
principle in particular has caused considerable controversy
ever since and is the apparent excuse for a great deal of human
rights' antagonism. Yet it is surely obviously logical. What kind
of absolute protection from torture would allow governments
to send people to such treatment, whether by extradition,
deportation or otherwise, as long as they don't do the dirty
work themselves? Such reasoning would sanction Guantanamo
itself and even 'extraordinary rendition' – or, as we in the real
world call it, state-sponsored kidnap and torture.

As Orwell would have observed, euphemisms for the previously
unthinkable, and therefore unspeakable, became extremely popular with the US and UK governments in the years after 9/11. We've
touched on 'enemy combatants', a phrase designed to create a new
category of prisoner subject to neither the ordinary criminal law
nor those governing war, and 'rendition' (which refers neither to
singing nor wall plastering). We were also later to learn of 'waterboarding', which was not a seaside sport but the dark interrogation
practice of beginning to drown a suspect in order to extract information from him.

Back in 1997 and as a young Home Office lawyer, I worked
on a piece of legislation which probably would have passed
in similar form regardless of the outcome of the now famous
general election. It was designed to implement the Strasbourg
Court's judgment in the Chahal case by creating a tribunal
capable of balancing the requirements of legal scrutiny of immigration decisions with the need to protect national security.
Inevitably an imperfect compromise, the Special Immigration

Appeals Commission (SIAC) was born: a secret administrative commission rather than a court, from which the migrant, his lawyers, press and public would be excluded for much of the hearing at which time a 'Special (security-vetted) Advocate' appointed by the Attorney General would attempt to test the government's case against him 'in the interests of justice'.

The obvious flaw in this fudge is that the Special Advocate is not allowed to speak to or take instructions from the subject of the hearing once he has seen the secret intelligence in the case. Thus he has little or no idea of what the migrant might say in response to it and what their alibi or innocent explanation might be. So, for example, if the case against a Chakrabarti facing deportation were that she had been seen having break-fast with a known terrorist at a particular place on a particular day, it is highly unlikely that she or her lawyers would be told this vital specific allegation. No doubt the agencies would argue that to reveal this detail would somehow risk identifying the undercover agent or informant who ran the café or also attended breakfast as a mole within the terrorist cell. The obvi-ous problem however, is that if, say, Chakrabarti could indeed prove that this must be a case of mistaken identity, by being able to demonstrate that she was on the other side of the world, or in prison, or on the operating table at just the time of the alleged sighting, she won't have been afforded this pretty basic fair trial opportunity.

Indeed in one now notorious immigration case some years later, it turned out that the authorities were arguing that a par-ticular false passport had been used by two suspects in different parts of the world at exactly the same time. The mistake emerged only by a chance coincidence because the same Special Advocate had been appointed by the government in both cases and he remembered something about the false passport that was reminiscent of the earlier case and was then able to alert all concerned to the gaping hole in the Secretary of State's story. But such coincidences rarely arise and if, as would have been far more usual, a different vetted barrister had been appointed in the second deportation case, it would have been impossible to expose the potential injustice – the shroud of secrecy hanging over both the proceedings and past judgments of SIAC.

People argued that the SIAC model was at least a little fairer than the complete lack of any appeal system that was the case before *Chahal v UK and the Special Immigration Appeals Commission Act 1997*. One could also argue that in a classic immigration case, the secret matter in issue was ultimately one of Home Secretary discretion rather than the migrant's fundamental rights. By definition, non-nationals have no 'right of abode' in the United Kingdom and therefore enter and stay out of the goodness of the Home Department's heart. Where fundamental rights such as the rule against torture (Article 3) or the right to respect for your private and family life (Article 8 – perhaps because you have a British child or spouse who cannot be expected to move with you to your country of nationality) are engaged, the issues in question need not require resolution in secret.

Sadly, however, secrecy is contagious and once the authorities become used to the delights of unfair lopsided pseudo-courts, they are unlikely ever to want to subject themselves to proper legal accountability again, even in other contexts. Who wouldn't take the permanent advantage of a secret chat with a judge rather than equal treatment with a legal opponent, if they could get away with it? So the obvious creative wheeze in the UK after 9/11 was the attempt to replace centuries-old fair criminal trial traditions – where you know the case against you and face a public trial in front of your peers – with administrative law 'immigration-style' as a means of locking people up indefinitely without trial, charges or even a police interview. The legal fiction was that this, being applied only to foreigners, was immigration detention pending deportation. However, according to the government's own argument the migrants in question could not be deported on account of the likelihood that they would be tortured in their home countries. It was the equivalent of arresting a group of teenage suspects and then holding them indefinitely in a prison temporarily designated as a boarding school. Yes, school-age children can lawfully be compulsorily educated just as migrants can lawfully be detained pending removal from the territory, but that isn't the intention or reality of the situation and everyone knows it. This was internment plain and simple and as divisive and counterproductive to national unity, community cohesion and intelligence-gathering as it previously had been in Northern Ireland during the troubles.

The New Labour Attorney General Lord Goldsmith would come to refer to the Belmarsh policy enshrined in Part 4 of the Anti-Terrorism, Crime and Security Act 2001 – emergency legislation rushed on to the statute book in the few weeks leading up to Christmas of that year – as constituting a 'three-walled prison'. The inmates could not be deported by the government due to the rule against torture (as applied in Chahal), but they were free to leave voluntarily at any time as long as they were prepared to take their chances with the torturers back home. What a choice – between your own revolver and the firing squad.

The ultimate fiction and grand abuse of language was the 'War on Terror' itself. President Bush's speechwriters had gone to war with an abstract noun that was ever part of the human experience to create a 'long war', 'new normal' or permanent emergency. Obviously, to those in the middle of an actual war, that war self-evidently feels indefinite, as it is impossible to know precisely when it will end. At the height of the Blitz, Londoners had no idea when exactly the war would be over and normal life (including temporarily suspended rights and freedoms) could resume. And yet they knew that when that time came, they would be able to verify it with their own senses (the end of hostilities, the signing of a peace treaty). This could never be the case with a 'War on Terror' – the term first used by

President Bush in an address to a joint session of Congress on 20 September 2001, in the aftermath of the attacks on New York and Washington. This war might go on for centuries until a President Bush or Clinton the twenty-third or twenty-fourth promises that it might be over and victory secured with just one more push. And of course a permanent emergency is the most dangerous contradiction in terms, with its permanence making it no longer temporary or exceptional. It is instead a new way of living – much closer, ironically, to the terrorists' fantasy – without the rights, freedoms and values on which our society is supposed to be built and which in the darkest of times more than ever we need to guide us.

2

The Law of Unintended Consequences

One does not simply walk into Mordor. Its black gates are guarded by more than just Orcs. There is evil there that does not sleep. The great Eye is ever watchful. It is a barren wasteland riddled with fire, ash and dust. The very air you breathe is a poisonous fume.

— Boromir at the Council of Elrond

It was 2003 and the best-selling movie was *The Lord of the Rings: The Return of the King*. I was applying for promotion. I had been working as a lawyer at Liberty for two years and felt that I'd made my contribution within the limits of the organization as it was. When my predecessor announced his resignation, I was already in the running for a number of other jobs, but the opportunity to reshape Liberty and expand our reach and influence from the courtroom into the newsroom, living room and parliamentary chamber was irresistible. In truth, I was completely unqualified to lead a human rights organization in need of regeneration. A lawyer and civil servant by background, what on earth did I really know about management, fundraising and how to reach different audiences to resist bad policies and practices or make positive change?

But the birth of my son, almost exactly a year before, had changed the way I looked at the world. There was something about being the mother of a one-year-old that had a strange and profound effect on me. New mothers often say that they can no longer bear to watch news footage or charity adverts featuring sick or starving children. Parenthood didn't have this impact on me; it did, however, deepen and intensify my passion for human rights' work.

With a small boy to nurture, the need to protect the vulnerable now felt more real, less abstract and philosophical. And just as parents and grandparents ought, no doubt, to find a greater interest in the future of the physical environment, 'constitutional climate change' and the erosion of our rights and freedoms became graver concerns for me with a new stake in the world beyond my lifetime. I also experienced an unexpected feeling of empowerment. Perhaps because I had been so anxious about motherhood, as I began to feel that I could manage that – the most important job in the world – other challenges seemed lesser by comparison. Minor infant health scares and mad dashes from the office to the nursery and GP were after all as stressful and crucial as anything work could throw up.

I applied for the job of director and the then board of Liberty was 'brave' enough to give it to me. I remember the mixed feeling of excitement, responsibility and anxiety on being promoted. I knew that the task would be significant and the support less so. I'd already been working at Liberty as a lawyer for two years but this made field research even more important – your first impression of anything is priceless and quickly disintegrates with loyalty, self-congratulation and introspection. So I spent a fair while talking to people inside and beyond the human rights movement about what we needed to be. In fact 'movement' is perhaps an exaggerated description of the rag bag of dissenters that we were at the time. The message was surprisingly consistent. 'You do lots of worthy legal work but where is the campaigning?'

For me, newly installed as Liberty's head, this came as something of a surprise. As a former law student and government lawyer, I had come to know the National Council for Civil Liberties and Liberty for its famous test-case litigation in both domestic and European Human Rights courts – and all my work for Liberty to date had been in this context. It was difficult to imagine what this romantic 'campaigning' ideal looked like.

Some of those I spoke with might have enjoyed the nostalgia and kinship of sitting in a room above a pub wherever they happened to live, talking to local like-minded people about the demise of age-old values. Others thought that marches and protests would do the trick almost by themselves; a view that brought many to disillusionment after the mass demonstrations that did not prevent the Iraq War. Others still understood that if violations of civil liberties and human rights could be expressed only if and when arguably illegal, there would be no language, let alone tools left in the locker, for laws, policies, decisions and actions that were just plain wrong.

After much soul-searching I came to the untested but, with hindsight, perhaps completely obvious view that what was needed was not to abandon the law and the courts as the back-stop of human rights protection, but instead to combine legal casework with advocacy in Parliament, the news media and wider civil discourse. How could we influence and convince if all we did was converse with the law?

We needed to reconnect with our historical roots in protest but also to reach beyond obvious allies and 'usual suspects' – to build new coalitions with democrats across the political spectrum in a world changed by technology and globalization but nonetheless plagued by challenges and abuses of power that would have been all too familiar to our founders in 1934.

This was all very well in theory – but it required a big change of approach on our part. When there's so much injustice around every corner, priorities become even more important for a small group of mostly young idealistic souls. A first-rate reactive law centre and press office were no longer enough. We had somehow to grow into a truly multi-disciplinary team of campaigning professionals, pooling our energies and pointing in the same direction. The first test and opportunity came very quickly indeed.

It was September 2003 and my first week officially in post as Liberty's director. London's Docklands area was hosting a now famous (or notorious) annual arms fair. Since 2001, the cavernous Excel Centre has biannually held the Defence Security and Equipment International exhibition. Unsurprisingly, anti-armaments campaigners had made it a focus for protest and were out in force. That September, the protests felt all the more significant given that the British government had embarked upon a controversial war in Iraq just six months earlier. Suddenly what seemed like every telephone in our grotty South London office began to ring. All the callers were saying the same thing: demonstrators were being barred from getting anywhere near the Excel Centre. Metropolitan Police officers were using anti-terror powers to stop and search and even arrest activists. To the brand new director of Liberty–NCCL, it seemed like 1934 all over again.

I asked colleagues to try to verify the information about the police's behaviour. The statute book is littered with public order and ordinary police powers with which officers can disrupt or prevent criminal or rowdy behaviour by protesters. Surely anti-terror powers were not being abused in a country with our proud tradition of dissent? We called the Metropolitan Police press office which flatly denied that these powers were being used – yet claims to the contrary kept on flooding in. So my colleague Alex Gask (then an aspiring lawyer, now a distinguished barrister in his own right) got quite literally on his bike to investigate. He returned a few hours later with a pile of notices issued by officers under Section 44 of the Terrorism Act 2000. Section 44 allows any area in the country to be defined as one where the police can stop and search any vehicle or person and seize 'articles of a kind which could be used in connection with terrorism'. Unlike with other stop and search powers, officers did not need to have 'reasonable suspicion' that an offence had been committed. Here was evidence that directly contradicted the initial denials by the police.

Our story was covered by the media and we threatened legal action. Twenty-four hours later, Members of Parliament began to express consternation. However, as is so often the case, their focus was in the main limited to the apparently outrageous *use* of a power by the police rather than in searching their own souls about why they crafted and passed such a bad and dangerous law in the first place.

This piece of legislation was not a response to 9/11 — in fact the Terrorism Act 2000 came into force a full six months before 9/11 and had been scrutinized and passed by both Houses of Parliament before that. It replaced 'temporary' Prevention of Terrorism legislation that had been passed and annually renewed since 1989 in the context of the troubles in Northern Ireland. This in itself should serve as an object lesson in how the state gains and rarely gives up power over the people and the ease with which temporary measures become permanent fixtures over time. The first thing to point out is the breathtakingly broad definition of 'terrorism' that is provided in its first section and that remains on the statute book to this day. At its broadest, it can catch threats as well as actions against property as well as people for the purpose of advancing a political or ideological cause.

It is practically a cliché – but no less true for that – to suggest that one man's terrorist is another's freedom fighter or even mere activist, and so it's obviously dangerous to peg anti-terror laws to ideological motivation rather than violent action. I am not as great a purist as those who say there should be no concept of terrorism at all. But surely it should be characterized not by the pursuit of someone's cause, but by his or her willingness to adopt 'any means necessary' and give up all respect for human life in the process (e.g. by inflicting death, torture or serious violence on innocents who get in the way). Instead our legislators had settled on a definition broad enough to catch a political graffiti artist or anti-GM crop protester who sprinkles non-GM seeds into a GM field. The fact that they are attempting to achieve political change now turns minor criminal damage or, some would say, mere nuisance or irritation into a terrorist offence.

When you combine this with the kind of speech crime laws that are considered appropriate to prosecute those who incite or 'glorify' terrorism, you have the prospect of catching someone who gives a speech in London to the effect that a brutal dictatorship on the other side of the world may, in the end, only be brought down by force. But it was the stop and search power in section 44 that came to prove one of the first and most graphic examples of the unintended consequences that flow from sloppy gung-ho legislation.

I accept that a police power to stop and search (in the US 'stop and frisk') is a necessary evil in any democratic society. The paradigm for such a power would be one triggered by 'reasonable suspicion' that the person to be stopped has just done or is about to do something wicked or is carrying a dangerous and illegal item on his or her person. Even this threshold of reasonable suspicion can prove an inadequate safeguard against abuse and discrimination. Police officers are human and therefore have human frailties such as gender, racial and age-based stereotyping in particular. Hence the tendency to single out young black men, even when a power is circumscribed in this way.

Equally, there are moments and places where waiting for reasonable suspicion of a particular person is an inadequate safety measure. So when I go through security at an airport or into the Houses of Parliament I have no problem with the automatic bag and body check. Why not? Because I understand that this place is likely to be a terrorist target and so the routine search is proportionate to the threat and, crucially, I don't feel singled out or discriminated against because of my race or politics. This is the kind of approach that can in principle justify a special anti-terror stop and search power. One can understand, for example, that, especially in the light of intelligence, it might be perfectly proportionate to cordon off the whole of Parliament Square on the day of the Opening of Parliament and require anyone who wants to enter to go through polite security screening. The same might apply to a high-profile sporting or other ceremonial occasion, especially where there is intelligence of a possible specific threat.

However, the drafting of the now-infamous section 44 was far too sloppy. It allowed a chief constable to designate an 'area' – which was not defined or limited by the statute – for stop and search without suspicion if it was 'expedient' (not even 'necessary') for fighting terrorism. No parliamentary or judicial authorization was required. The designations lasted up to twenty-eight days at a time and the only so-called safeguard was the Home Secretary's retrospective endorsement. It was only during the test case that Liberty subsequently brought against the Docklands operation, on behalf of journalist Penny Quinton and protester Kevin Gillan, that we learned that the entire Metropolitan Police area (the whole of Greater London) had been designated on a rolling twenty-eight-day basis for eighteen months before the incident and ever since the legislation had come into force. Like some hideous dystopian sci-fi story, our great capital city had been turned into a stop and search zone.

While we made some progress in the domestic courts, and not for the first time, it took the European Court of Human Rights in Strasbourg (including judges from younger and rockier democracies less complacent than we sometimes are about the risk of abuse of state power) over six years to find in January 2010 that section 44 was so broad as to violate the right to respect for private life enshrined in Article 8 of the Human Rights Convention. The court said that:

... the powers of authorization and confirmation as well as those of stop and search ... are neither sufficiently circumscribed nor subject to adequate legal safeguards against abuse ... They are not therefore 'in accordance with the law'.

This historic Liberty victory was an indictment indeed of our politicians. The anti-terror stop and search power that they had waved through before even the maelstrom of 9/11 was so lax and devoid of safeguards for the citizen that it did not constitute proper law. When is a door not a door? When it's ajar. When is a law not a law? When it's a political speech or press release masquerading as properly thought-through legislation.

It was to take six years to get our challenge all the way to final judgment in the Court of Human Rights and not before the law had been abused at the expense of many more young black men and peaceful dissenters alike. In 2005, section 44 was invoked at the Labour Party conference in Brighton to haul the octogenarian Holocaust survivor Walter Wolfgang out of the auditorium, forcing Tony Blair to apologize on national television. Walter's crime was a gentle heckle of the then Foreign Secretary – and my old Home Office boss – Jack Straw as he gave his platform speech. In a vibrant democracy, should senior national politicians really be protected from a little heckling any more than stand-up comedians are? Shouldn't they welcome a small challenge as a vital occupational hazard to be proud of?

During the height of the Iraq War, whole counties of England and Wales were designated for stop and search without suspicion – just as all of Greater London was secretly designated on a rolling basis from 2001. If you go back to my airport or Palace of Westminster analogy, a designation on that scale cannot possibly be used against everyone in the area and can instead only become a tool of discrimination or oppression against peaceful dissent or young black and Asian men in particular. Indeed the official statistics for 2007–8 revealed that only

0.6 per cent of these searches ever led to an arrest, let alone a criminal charge, and that black and Asian people were between five and seven times more likely to be stopped under section 44. This fact was not lost on the much-maligned Court of Human Rights. In 2010 the coalition government replaced and tightened up the power, introducing greater safeguards against abuse by accident or design, but two similar and equally divisive provisions remain untouched.

Often it takes the implementation, rather than the passing of badly thought-out laws to bring them to public attention and to provoke a concerted response. Just as it took the suppression of the hunger marches to induce the birth of NCCL–Liberty in 1934 and the arms fair affair in 2003 to expose section 44 to greater public gaze, the power in Schedule 7 of the same Terrorism Act of 2000 failed to attract any real public or political attention until it was used in 2013 to detain David Miranda (the partner of a *Guardian* journalist who had worked with the whistleblower Edward Snowden in exposing the scale of blanket internet surveillance on entire populations by the US and UK security communities). Prior to the Miranda incident (and how appropriate that David should share his surname with the Miranda of the US test case that led to people being read their rights on arrest) the power to detain without suspicion people (including British nationals) coming into the United Kingdom for up to nine hours had been almost exclusively used against Muslim passengers.

And while it is a positive development that section 44 has been tightened, the similar power contained in ordinary policing legislation for dealing with gun and knife crime rather than terrorism is subject to even lower-level internal police authorization and remains on the statute book to harass and alienate generation after generation of young black men in our inner cities, creating an instinctive suspicion of or even hostility to the police force that ought to provide a comfort or even a career opportunity for the law-abiding and public-spirited young.

Yet if powers passed even before the War on Terror could lead to such unexpected, unfortunate and counterproductive results, what of those passed after the Twin Towers atrocity when fear stalked the land on both sides of the Atlantic?

Extradition is surely an obvious case in point. This is the process by which the authorities of one country send a suspect or defendant who faces charges in another to face trial in the place where he has allegedly offended or where it is otherwise most obvious that he should be dealt with. No one, as far as I can tell, has ever credibly argued for a world where escaping across an international border 'train robbers' style' should allow someone to escape justice from those they may have wronged. Yet to be taken from your work, family, community, language and legal system to another country where they do things differently, and where you may have never voted, let alone offended, and where you will most likely not get bail in the months or years pending trial, can be a punishment in itself for someone who we need to remember is to be presumed innocent at this stage in the process. So certain legal safeguards should surely be in place to minimize the dangers to the innocent.

Surely no one should be taken from their home on the basis of a charge that doesn't even amount to a crime in the country where they now live? To prevent ripping people from their lives on trumped-up charges, a basic case should surely be made out to a judge in a local court before the accused are sent to face trial in another country? And if a significant part of the alleged offending conduct took place at home (as with crimes involving the internet, where you need not have left your computer let alone the country), a local court should have the discretion to decide whether it is in the best interests of justice that you be sent abroad or considered for prosecution by the authorities here in the UK.

To be fair, prior to 9/11, extradition had become a long-winded and convoluted process, but babies and bath-water come to mind in the context of what happened next. The New Labour government signed up to a new one-sided treaty with the United States, allowing people in the United Kingdom to be sent over there for trial with little more than a by your leave, while Americans, with their entrenched constitutional protections, remained entitled to some scrutiny of the case against them in a US court before being extradited over here. Then there was the European Arrest Warrant, agreed within nine months of the atrocity, which would effectively treat the European Union as one federal state for the purposes of extradition, but without harmonizing the criminal laws or police station and fair trial protections first.

I am an internationalist, not least because I believe human rights to be universal and human beings to be of equal worth and entitled to protection whatever the accidents of birth, history and geography. So I can hardly speak against greater international cooperation between the governments of our shrinking planet. Yet it seems telling that the cooperation that they espouse is so often one of governmental and administrative convenience, while they simultaneously undermine universal human rights protections agreed by democrats across the globe after the Holocaust and the Blitz.

Challenges and threats whether posed by crime or our changing environment are global and so our responses must be international as well. Yet the individual human being cannot be so much lost in this equation that human rights and legitimate participatory democracy vanish from the process.

If we were robots or supermarket products, summary or instant extradition wouldn't matter as long as we could be sure of a fair trial at the end of it. But of course, we are neither androids nor sacks of carrots and to be taken from your home, job, family and community, away from your supporters, advisers and quite possibly language and legal system as well, to be detained in a foreign jail for months on end as a 'fugitive offender', can be punishment in itself whatever happens next.

The practical and psychological pressure to trade a guilty plea for the promise of a lenient sentence or the opportunity to serve it out back home can prove irresistible, particularly in a country without legal aid and where the costs of defending yourself against political prosecutors out to prove a point could cost you your home and any savings you have.

There is also the question of the 'legitimacy' of the law and why we feel bound by it. In a democracy, one obvious reason is that, particularly as adults of voting age, we have a democratic stake in the political community that created it (whether we actually voted for or agreed with the specific law in question). When we travel to another country, there is an element of '... when in Rome' and playing by the house rules of another land where we are to considerable extent a guest. But what if you never left your own home or office, let alone your country, but find yourself subject to the tentacles of the authorities of a foreign power, most likely because of your activities on the internet over which legislators and enforcers assert authority across oceans and continents? What stake and say could you have in your subsequent treatment, particularly if universal human rights (as opposed to the rights and privileges of citizens) are not respected and even undermined?

Then there is the question of whose idea of that wonderful flexible friend 'the public interest' is being considered. Extradition law and practice can be a strange cocktail of domestic and international law and politics. In some countries (for example some in Europe) there is theoretically a duty on prosecutors to enforce against every breach of the criminal law. It is a strange notion to those of us in the common law world, and one feels sure it cannot be applied universally in practice. In other jurisdictions closer to our own, prosecutors look not just at the evidence in the case and the elements of the criminal offence but at the public interest in taking matters further.

This can mean considering the balance between the seriousness of the offence and the practical and financial costs of prosecution and the best use of resources. Also and crucially, it can involve a closer, humane and discretionary examination of the circumstances of the alleged offender and indeed any victims and families. So it is this public interest discretion (around which the Director of Public Prosecutions will from time to time set out guidelines) that, for example, allows some assisted suicides or even mercy killings of the terminally ill and debilitated to go unpunished in our country, even though there has been no formal change in the law of homicide to deal with these incredibly difficult cases.

Further, the vulnerability and other circumstances of the alleged offender can be relevant. However, all too sadly, it isn't just in our own country that the public interest in compassion over vengeance seems less compelling when the authorities are dealing with a foreign national rather than someone with local community or national support. How easily may bilateral treaties, and even domestic statutes passed in the name of dealing with terrorists, be employed in completely surprising ways?

The first *cause célèbre* under the Extradition Act 2003 involved the so-called 'NatWest Three' (despite attempts by US and UK authorities to rebrand the defendants as the 'Enron Three' in an obvious attempt to hype the case and assert the legitimacy of American jurisdiction). Three British businessmen – David Bermingham, Giles Darby and Gary Mulgrew – were accused by US prosecutors of defrauding their former employer, NatWest, out of more than $7 million. They denied the charges and NatWest itself never made any allegations against them. The US authorities waited for the new Extradition Act 2003 to come into force, in January 2004, before seeking the trio's extradition. Despite being British citizens, living in London, accused of defrauding a British bank also based in London, the men faced the prospect of being hauled across the Atlantic, away from their families and loved ones, to face trial. And, under the new Act, the UK courts were unable to bar such removals, even when the conduct leading to the alleged criminal activity had taken place here. The trio, supported by my Liberty colleagues and a broad campaign to which the irrepressible Digby Jones (then of the CBI and now a cross-bench peer) lent his voice, pushed hard for the introduction of a new 'Forum' clause that would force prosecutors to make the case for extradition before a UK court first. That amendment was supported by the Conservatives and Liberal Democrats (in opposition at the time), but defeated by the Labour government.

Charles Clarke, the then Home Secretary, endorsed the Nat-West Three's extradition in May 2005. The men appealed to the High Court – a case in which we at Liberty intervened – but lost after the government argued that honouring international extradition treaties must come first. Despite growing public support for halting the trio's extradition, the government claimed there was nothing it could do and the men were sent to the US in July 2006. After being unable to access witnesses or documents from Texas, they entered into a plea bargain in November 2007 in exchange for a promise of repatriation. In February 2008 they were each sentenced to thirty-seven months in prison. They were first jailed in the US before returning to the UK to serve the remainder of their sentences.

David Bermingham, a former law student and army officer, went on to write his own powerful story about his experiences, *A Price to Pay*. One of the many things that surprised me about this episode was the way in which some journalists, commentators and even members of the legal community found it so hard to see past the privileged lives and high-octane City lifestyle that these men had once enjoyed to the fundamental dangers and unfairness of the politics and process they were being subjected to. My friend and stalwart campaigner for fair extradition Melanie Riley was also sometimes attacked because of her role as a public relations professional. All I can say about that is that we can all choose to use our skills for our beliefs as well as for money, and *pro bono* campaigning by someone who usually makes their living at it seems no less laudable to me than *pro bono* advice and representation from a lawyer in private practice. Melanie continues to campaign in this area and has helped many of those facing summary extradition regardless of their race, religion or financial circumstances.

Meanwhile, retired British businessman Christopher Tappin found himself at the mercy of our extradition arrangements after being accused of conspiracy to export missile parts from the US to Iran. It was part of a 'sting' operation set up by US immigration and customs enforcement officials. Mr Tappin insisted he was merely a freight provider – arranging the shipping of industrial batteries from Texas to the Netherlands. Again, the evidence against him was never tested in a British court. There was no judicial discretion allowed as to whether Mr Tappin's case might be better served by a trial in the UK. Instead he too faced being flown thousands of miles from home, away from his sick wife, despite the fact that all of the allegations were connected to conduct on British soil. Mr Tappin's extradition was ordered by the Home Secretary in April 2011. In January 2012, he lost his final appeal against removal to the US under the Extradition Act. The following month, he was handed to US marshals and put on a flight to El Paso in Texas.

I will never forget appearing on a popular phone-in radio programme that same lunchtime. The interviewer played me a recording of Mr Tappin's final public comments before boarding the aeroplane at Heathrow airport. He was understandably upset and remarked on how unfair he thought it was that the Jordanian terror suspect Abu Qatada could not be deported for fear he would be tortured in his own country, while Tappin was being bundled off from Britain. I certainly understood his anguish but attempted to remind listeners of the ease with which any one of us might be seen as a 'foreign terror suspect' in another land. Out in Texas, Christopher Tappin was not going to be viewed as a pillar of his local community, but as a foreigner accused of arming Iran. In Texas then, he would look somewhat like Mr Qatada could seem to British eyes. Following difficulties in mounting a defence, including getting witnesses to testify in the US, Mr Tappin pleaded guilty after reaching an agreement with prosecutors. He spent six months in jail in Pennsylvania before returning to the UK to serve the remainder of his sentence.

Computer expert Babar Ahmad, from South London, was accused, along with Talha Ahsan, of setting up terrorist fundraising websites, and detained for eight years without charge. Again the alleged criminal conduct took place here in the UK, but again the authorities refused to prosecute Mr Ahmad here – or allow a private prosecution attempted by the businessman Karl Watkin – and set about facilitating the accused's extradition to the US. Again, the serious impact of extradition on Mr Ahmad and his family – not to mention the inevitable difficulties involved in prosecuting the crime in the US, with many of the witnesses and much of the evidence being in the UK – were ignored. Had the evidence passed to the US been properly considered by the CPS, it was highly likely there would have been sufficient material to charge Mr Ahmad and place him on trial in Britain. But that never happened and, after a lengthy legal battle, both the European Court of Human Rights, in April 2012, and the UK High Court, the following October, ruled that Mr Ahmad could be lawfully extradited to the US to face terrorism charges. In December 2013, he pleaded guilty before a court in Connecticut. It was difficult to see how such outsourcing of justice under our lax extradition laws would do anything for the public's trust in British law enforcement.

Thankfully some victims of our rotten system have escaped extradition. Sheffield student Richard O'Dwyer was able to reach an agreement with US prosecutors to avoid his removal – but not before a desperate two-year legal battle, led by his mother Julia. Richard was accused of copyright infringement by US authorities for hosting a website, TVShack, offering links to downloadable pirate films and TV shows. Not actual content – just *links*. He built the site from his Sheffield bedroom, and his computer server was not even based in the US. Yet still Richard faced being hauled across the Atlantic to stand trial. His extradition order was approved by the Home Secretary (by then Theresa May) despite the Conservatives and the Liberal Democrats committing to extradition reform while in opposition. In January 2012, Westminster magistrates ruled that Richard could be extradited to the US on piracy charges – another reminder of just how unfair our extradition laws had become. Mercifully, in November 2012, it was announced that an agreement had been reached and that all charges had been dropped. Richard's case, like the others', underlined the need for our extradition arrangements to be overhauled to allow people who have never even left our shores to be dealt with here at home. Only urgent legislation can prevent similar torment in future.

But perhaps the most famous case to emerge since the introduction of the Extradition Act 2003 is that of Gary McKinnon. He is the British man who was charged with hacking into US Pentagon and NASA systems between 1999 and 2002. For ten long years, Gary faced the threat of extradition to the US in order to stand trial. He was diagnosed with a form of autism known as Asperger's syndrome and his lawyers argued in an appeal to the European Court of Human Rights that, because of this and given that the crime was committed on British soil, he should be tried in the UK. Regrettably, the court refused to intervene and Gary lived for a decade with the prospect of sixty years in a US jail hanging over him.

However, in October 2012 the Home Secretary Theresa May announced her refusal to extradite Gary on human rights grounds. Her decision came after a report by Home Office-appointed psychiatrists warned that Gary would very likely attempt suicide if sent for trial across the Atlantic. The sparing of this vulnerable man was a great day for rights, freedoms and justice in the UK and a testament to the campaign supporting him, led by his fearless mother Janis Sharp. Janis, like my dear friend Doreen Lawrence, should be an inspiration to mothers and campaigners everywhere. These great women didn't go to law school as I did and then take the path of human rights as a professional and political choice. Tragically, they had no choice and when others, perhaps myself included, would have crumbled in the face of such enormous adversity, they converted their love and responsibility towards their own children into broader campaigns for other people's children and generations to come. It has been a privilege to sit beside these women at important moments in their lives.

Janis's was a fight that united lawyers, politicians, press and the public from across the spectrum in the cause of compassion and common sense. But the Home Secretary gives and she also takes away. Subsequent Home Office legislation removed the very same compassionate power that had allowed her to help Gary.

Theresa May announced that the law would be changed to introduce the 'Forum Bar' – the reform which we at Liberty had long called for. This, we hoped, would mean that British courts would be allowed to bar extradition where the alleged conduct has taken place, in whole or in part, in the UK and it is in the interests of justice to do so. Had such a law been in force when Gary's case first came before the courts, his extradition could have been barred on this basis and he would not have had to wait so long.

Frustratingly, there is already a provision that would achieve precisely this, which has laid dormant on the statute book since 2006. But, rather than activate it, the government brought forward new legislation which fell well short of the mark. Rather than giving judges the ability to consider what the interests of justice demand in a case where the activity complained of took place in this country, the Crime and Courts Act makes provision for what is little more than a nominal discretion. Judges' hands are tied by the inclusion of a prescriptive list of consid-erations, all of which skew the balance in favour of extradition. Perhaps more concerning still, no consideration can be given to barring extradition in cases where a decision has been made not to prosecute in the UK. Not much help to the Gary McKin-nons and the Richard O'Dwyers who were not facing prosecution at home. Perversely however, those whose alleged conduct is capable of amounting to serious offending in this country can avail themselves of this albeit very limited discre-tion. At Liberty, we will continue to call on the coalition government to honour its vow, and the principles both parties strongly supported while in opposition, by making meaningful changes to our extradition system. Extradition should prevent fugitives escaping – not allow for people like Gary to be par-celled off around the world based on allegations of offences committed here at home.

So what did I learn from stop and search and summary extradition as well as other bad, sloppily conceived laws? I learned that if you don't speak up for the terror suspect, there may be no one to speak up for you and that politicians' prom ises won't even come close to hard-edged legal human rights protection when it's you or a loved one who is in trouble.

3

Charge or Release

'*Does Magna Carta mean nothing to you? Did she die in vain?*'

– from 'Twelve Angry Men', BBC TV Series
5 of *Hancock's Half Hour* (first broadcast
16 October 1959)

By December 2004 I had been officially in post for fifteen months. These were tumultuous days in British politics. After months of media scrutiny of his private life the Home Secretary David Blunkett resigned on 15 December. He was accused of helping to fast-track a visa for his ex-partner's nanny. Mr Blunkett was the first Home Secretary I encountered as director of Liberty (having worked for Michael Howard and then Jack Straw as a Home Office lawyer). With hindsight, Blunkett's instincts were probably no more authoritarian than those of his two immediate predecessors. But when he assumed office in 2001 and was faced almost immediately with 9/11 he grasped the moment as one of political opportunity rather than ethical dilemma. The forced destitution of asylum seekers, the grand folly of identity cards and the Belmarsh internment policy were introduced with gusto on his watch.

Unsurprisingly, my colleagues and I had a lot of contact with Blunkett. In my dealings with him, I found him courteous, but at times when we had been vocal in our criticisms of his approach, his faintly menacing special adviser would send portentous emails late in the evening. We were ridiculed as the 'liberati' with 'airy fairy' concerns about rights and freedoms. This latter phrase was later parroted by Conservative Prime Minister David Cameron in the context of the mass surveillance by our security agencies. Moreover, the judiciary, even particular judges, were castigated for sometimes ruling against the Home Office in legal challenges. Once he stopped drinking the Home Office Kool–Aid, Blunkett came to show some sensitivity and even regret about summary extradition and aspects of data retention in particular. (All irony notwithstanding, my liberal heart bled more than a little at the personal intrusions he suffered at the time.) However, it was his thoughtful and subtler successor, Charles Clarke, who inherited the mother of all hangovers and an in-tray full of splitting headaches. On his first day in office, 16 December 2004, the Law Lords – the judges of the highest court in the land – finally ruled on the post-9/11 policy of interning foreign terror suspects without charge or trial indefinitely in Belmarsh Prison. Eight out of nine judges found these procedures incompatible with the Human Rights Convention. By this time seven of the claimants had been detained without so much as a police interview for three years each. Those suspected of recruiting them – British nationals all – remained uncharged under the criminal law of the land and lived their lives at liberty. And here, in this disproportionate and irrational discrimination, lay the rub.

The European Convention on Human Rights is the child neither of nineteenth-century legal purity nor of 1960s hippy liberalism, so often derided by Tony Blair and too many of his colleagues when in office. Rather, it was drafted in the aftermath of the Second World War, when enemy aliens in the form of German and Japanese citizens had been interned by Allied powers on both sides of the Atlantic. Its rulings carry the echoes of a world still recovering from conflict. Although the

Convention absolutely and unequivocally condemns torture and slavery, most rights and freedoms stipulated in it are qualified. Even the rights to liberty and to a fair trial may be curtailed or 'derogated' from in a 'time of war or other public emergency threatening the life of the nation'. This is a tradition that in England can be traced back to Magna Carta. This curtailment can only happen, though, 'in so far as is strictly necessary'.

Two months after 9/11, Blair and Blunkett authorized such a 'derogation' from the Convention. This was a gesture that many saw as an act of symbolic solidarity with the cages of President Bush's Guantanamo. In both cases non-nationals only were interned. But while the US government was able to circumvent its own Bill of Rights by maintaining that it applied only to American citizens, and that Guantanamo, as an offshore jurisdiction outside US territory, was beyond the bill's reach, this was never going to work in the UK where the ECHR is built upon universal rights contingent on humanity not nationality. It was drawn up in the immediate and shocking knowledge of how the European Jews had been deprived of the 'privilege' of nationality in the 1930s and 40s and in the belief that whatever the whims of the powerful – and even of political majorities – humanity should never again be so easily cast aside.

You will remember the legal fiction that this was 'immigration detention' in a 'three-walled prison'. You are free to leave at any time to take your chances with the torturers back home. This was created to avoid the charge of illogical and unlawful discrimination against foreign national terror suspects. In order to get the derogation approved, Blair and Blunkett went out of their way to embroider the 2001 legislation with apparent safeguards against oppression. A Home Office appointee scrutinized the working of this 'exceptional measure'. A long-standing Liberal Democrat peer, he called himself the 'independent', rather than the 'Statutory' or 'Home Office' reviewer. There were lopsided appeals to the secret SIAC tribunal as a saccharine substitute for habeas corpus and judicial review in open court.

From the time of its introduction in 2001, Liberty had campaigned relentlessly against this policy in Parliament, the media, the courts and civil society. Others would come only much later to the victory party when it was easy, fashionable and more popular to do so. When the bill was first published, we commissioned an opinion from David Pannick QC, highly respected in government circles. Pannick advised Parliament that, however horrific the 9/11 attacks had been, they did not constitute a 'threat to the life of (our) nation' – that is, the UK. In his view the proposed exception to the Human Rights Convention was unwarranted. What was more, the illogical and discriminatory nature of the proposed internment provisions could not possibly meet the second test of 'strict necessity' required for a lawful derogation. I will never forget telephoning David from Liberty's ramshackle former offices in South London, just as I had done from the mighty Home Office on so many occasions before. This time there was no brief fee or carefully prepared bundle of manicured instructions on offer, but his response was as professional and enthusiastic as ever. 'Come and see me with whatever papers you have this afternoon,' he said. 'Don't worry, Shami. Always ask a busy person.'

As the legislation proceeded through Parliament, we convened a small group of the private practice lawyers most likely to represent those affected. The most prominent of these was the legendary terror trial lawyer Gareth Peirce, of whom I was in considerable awe. Peirce was renowned for her work representing alleged IRA defendants such as the Birmingham Six and Guildford Four, righting a number of actual and potential miscarriages of justice in the process.

Three things struck me from my early encounters with this iconic campaigning solicitor and bulwark against complacency in our legal establishment. Firstly, her courage and experience are exceeded only by her personal and intellectual humility: she was more than willing to collaborate with relative litigation novices and unknowns like me. Secondly, her radical beliefs sat perfectly comfortably alongside a street-smart wisdom and loyalty to her clients' best interests. Unlike many others at the time, she never seemed suspicious of this youngish former Home Officer lawyer, but was genuinely intrigued by the different insights and experience that I might bring to the struggle. Finally – and perhaps most significantly – Gareth was genuinely aghast at the draft provisions of what would become Part 4 of the Anti-Terrorism, Crime and Security Act 2001, as the Belmarsh legislation was technically known. How could such an experienced lawyer, who had seen much prejudice and injustice in the context of anti-terror law, be shocked? The answer was relatively simple. Even the anti-terror legislation of the 1970s and 80s, with its limitations on solicitor access, reverse burdens of proof and broad drafting, bore some distorted semblance to the ordinary criminal law, with some kind of trial to follow in due course at the Old Bailey. Not so under 'administrative law' and the fiction of 'immigration detention' in particular. This genuine consternation from a great legal veteran where there could so easily have been cynicism was as inspiring as it was humbling to the former Home Office hack that I had been.

So Gareth represented the 'detainees', another War on Terror euphemism, this time for people who had been imprisoned without trial. She represented them at all three levels of appeal and Liberty 'intervened' as a third party in the public interest. Liberty's role was, and remains, particularly significant in this regard. Individual claimants are not always best placed to make broader public-interest or policy arguments, particularly with decimated legal aid provision and in the face of arrogant and sweeping government arguments about the greater good in general and public safety in particular. It was a role that would become increasingly important in human rights litigation as government sought to trump the rights of 'the few' – foreign nationals, suspects or particular communities – with the supposed rights 'of the many', whether in the context of privacy, liberty or, subsequently, even torture.

Despite Liberty's efforts, the Court of Appeal accepted the Blair government's 'Bill of Goods' about emergency, necessity and immigrants being 'different' from the 'law-abiding majority'. The House of Lords, though, did not. Instead, it protected our modern Bill of Rights in thought, word and deed. Of the nine Law Lords who sat on the appeal, one found with the government. Of the remaining eight, one found against the government even on the delicate issue of whether an 'emergency or threat to the life of the nation' existed at all on account of 9/11. Lord Hoffmann noted that:

> This is a nation which has been tested in adversity, which has survived physical destruction and catastrophic loss of life. I do not underestimate the ability of fanatical groups of terrorists to kill and destroy, but they do not threaten the life of the nation. Whether we would survive Hitler hung in the balance, but there is no doubt that we shall survive Al-Qaeda. The Spanish people have not said that what happened in Madrid, hideous crime as it was, threatened the life of their nation. Their legendary pride would not allow it. Terrorist violence, serious as it is, does not threaten our institutions of government or our existence as a civil community.

> ... The real threat to the life of the nation, in the sense of a people living in accordance with its traditional laws and political values, comes not from terrorism but from laws such as these. That is the true measure of what terrorism may achieve. It is for Parliament to decide whether to give the terrorists such a victory.*

* Lord Hoffmann, from paragraphs 96 and 97 of *A and Others v Secretary of State for the Home Department*

This may have been Lord Hoffmann's most lyrical hour. Naturally, my Liberty colleagues and I agreed with him, to the extent of taking out a full-page newspaper advert the next day quoting his final eloquent flourish about the 'real threat to the life of the nation' under the banner: 'Guantanamo Bay – closer than you think'. By doing this, we were urging the government to reflect and amend the shameful, unjust and counterproductive law. On reflection, what the majority of Law Lords did was more astute. They effectively deferred to the government on the issue of the nature of any emergency that may or may not have existed. Judges, after all, are not – and in my view should not be – privy to any secret intelligence assessments that are not made available for scrutiny by the press, public, prisoners and suspects.

Instead the majority relied on the cold forensic legal logic that senior judges do so much better than politicians and campaigners. Whatever the intelligence assessment or debate about whether a particular threat can be called an emergency, the discrimination argument was inescapable and effortlessly non-political in its reasoning.

The Attorney General submitted that the position of the appellants should be compared with that of non-UK nationals who represented a threat to the security of the UK but who could be removed to their own or to safe third countries. The relevant difference between them and the appellants was that the appellants could not be removed. A difference of treatment between the two groups was accordingly justified and it was reasonable and necessary to detain the appellants. By contrast, the appellants' chosen comparators were suspected international terrorists who were UK nationals. The appellants pointed out that they shared with this group the important characteristics a) of being suspected international terrorists and b) of being irremovable from the United Kingdom. Since these were the relevant characteristics for the purposes of the comparison, it was unlawfully discriminatory to detain non-UK nationals while leaving UK nationals at large.

Were suspected internationals who were UK nationals, the appellants' chosen comparators, in a relevantly analogous situation to the appellants? . . . In my opinion, the question demands an affirmative answer. Suspected international terrorists who are UK nationals are in a situation analogous with the appellants because, in the present context, they share the most relevant characteristics of the appellants . . . The comparison contended for by the Attorney General might be reasonable and justified in an immigration context, but cannot in my opinion be so in a security context, since the threat presented by international terrorists did not depend on their nationality or immigration status.*

A terrorist atrocity in London less than a year later would prove them absolutely right. When nations are not at war in the conventional sense and the battle is either one of ideology or pure victimhood, British nationals are just as capable of abomination as their foreign counterparts. A policy of interning foreign nationals only is irrational and discriminatory; it cannot therefore possibly be 'strictly necessary'.

I would add that discrimination, as much or more than any other profound injustice, results in a festering resentment that recruits more terrorists than it can ever prevent. In any event, the majority of Law Lords found the Belmarsh policy unlawful for its irrational and disproportionate discrimination, and my friend Gareth Peirce printed the Hoffmann quote that so riled the government on a T-shirt for my toddler: 'Dignity, equality and fairness and the greatest of these is equality.'

Their Lordships having opined, the ball was quite firmly in the government's court. And as I pointed out earlier, the Lords' 'declaration of incompatibility' under the Human Rights Act in respect of the Belmarsh legislation could only be moral and

* Lord Bingham, from paragraphs 52 to 54 of *A and Others v Secretary of State for the Home Department*

persuasive: it had no binding force. The declaration of incompatibility was reliant on our still sovereign Parliament to do the right thing and change the law.

The new Home Secretary, Charles Clarke, was lumbered with the quandary of how to respond to the Lords' declaration. For a while rumours, doubtless in the form of Number 10 briefings, abounded that Her Majesty's government might offer two fingers instead of an olive branch to her judges. While still in the Home Office, I had had the pleasure of advising Clarke when he was a Home Office minister of state and before his first elevation to the cabinet as Education Secretary. He was, I knew, smarter than to dismiss the judges' ruling out of hand – and so it proved. Instead, he despatched officials to recommend a new policy, one less offensive to the Law Lords' concerns of discrimination and disproportionality. Sadly the resulting legislation was a triumph of form over substance, as if a response to an intellectual puzzle with little to do in any real sense with either liberty or security.

Back in 1997, in the months after the general election when 'things could only get better', New Labour had drafted a new Crime and Disorder Bill in which the concept of anti-social behaviour first took legal rather than colloquial shape. Anti-social behaviour orders, or ASBOs, were championed in some progressive circles as a civil order offering a last chance for petty criminals to stay out of the criminal justice system. They could equally and more accurately be sold as a gung-ho means of summary punishment with no need for charges, evidence or proof.

ASBOs involved a definition of bad behaviour far vaguer and more sweeping than that provided by the criminal law: 'conduct which caused or is likely to cause harm, harassment, alarm or distress'. The police or local authority could apply for an ASBO and, if a magistrates' court was satisfied that this low threshold of concern had been met, it would grant an injunction with a wide range of conditions, breach of which constituted a criminal offence punishable with imprisonment.

ASBOs could create a bespoke and arbitrary criminal code for people who had never been proved to have breached the ordinary criminal law of the land. In the words of the Prime Minister, outlining his 'five-year plan on law and order' in July 2004: 'We asked the police what powers they wanted and we gave them to them.'

But in the copy and paste world of policy and legislation by numbers, the circumvention of criminal due process with civil orders was to find an even more chilling apotheosis. In 2005, the ASBO was crossed with the secret administrative procedure that was SIAC to produce the mutant creature that became the 'control order'. Now punishment without charge or trial would not even be based on hearsay and a magistrate's view of what might or might not constitute nuisance, but on secret intelligence and the Home Secretary's suspicions alone.

Control orders would apply to Britons and non-nationals alike, in an attempt to meet the Law Lords' concerns about discrimination. Further, they used not formal institutional imprisonment but house arrest, in order to seem more moderate and proportionate than, for example, internment in the notorious Belmarsh. In practical terms, however, these 'anti-terror ASBOs' provided neither safety nor freedom. As with the more common measures on which they were modelled, they were often and easily breached by those prepared to take the simple step of cutting off a plastic ankle tag in order to abscond. Yet they were capable of blighting the lives of the genuinely law abiding and their families, including small children, who also suffered a whole range of Home Office rather than court-ordered indignities, intrusions and restrictions on secret and unproven suspicions alone – with no need for a criminal charge or trial. Indeed, Gareth Peirce once pointed out that for some of her single male clients, including one who was quite significantly disabled and wheelchair-bound, institutional imprisonment would at least have provided some company and association rather than the solitary confinement of being kept home alone.

When the Prevention of Terrorism (Control Order) Bill was introduced in early 2005, it met with vocal opposition from both the left and right-of-centre of British politics and the press. The principal political opposition was led by the formidable Conservative team of Shadow Home Secretary David Davis and Shadow Attorney General Dominic Grieve. The Liberal Democratic leadership under Charles Kennedy appeared more distracted and less sure-footed, but nonetheless their rank-and-file membership were united in their belief in the right to a fair trial as a core liberal value. Indeed, Lib Dem leaders sometimes overlook the fact that while Labour and Conservative activists and voters often coalesce around their view of tax and spend and split almost 50/50 along the liberal–authoritarian axis, both political principle and polling suggest that liberals of both the left and right of the economic centre are likely to unite around a shared view of rights and freedoms despite disparate opinions on almost every other issue.

The most moving stand against control orders came from New Labour's own ranks during the House of Commons' second reading of the draft legislation. This was the first opportunity for MPs to debate the main principles of the bill. In a speech that made the hairs on the back of my neck stand on end, the now former MP for Stevenage, Barbara Follett, described the orders as having an 'extraordinary resemblance' to similar laws employed in apartheid South Africa and under which her first husband, Richard Turner, lived for five years for campaigning for the universal franchise in that country:

> House arrest hampered but didn't stop him . . . That is why, just before his five-year order was due to expire, he was shot dead in front of our two young daughters in their bedroom . . .
>
> In the days that followed I tried to comfort them by telling them we were going to Britain where people were not detained without trial or put under house arrest.

After a series of bruising defeats and essentially cosmetic concessions including the now entirely predictable presentational trick of co-opting the judiciary into a one-sided secret process, an exasperated Prime Minister Blair appeared on national television to warn opponents that 'enough was enough' and threatened to call a general election on the issue of control orders alone. Unsurprisingly, after such anti-democratic brinkmanship, the legislation then passed both houses without much further difficulty, the government appearing to cede ground in what was essentially a time-worn ruse. Typically, the government turned up to Parliament armed with pre-planned fall-back positions to which it always expected to have to resort without actually giving way on any of the planned legislation's fundamental points. Judicial bells, whistles and sugar-coating notwithstanding, so it proved: people subject to control orders would still be subject to lengthy curfews and other serious restrictions on their liberty on the basis of suspicion and secret intelligence that neither they nor their lawyers would ever be able to test.

And this was a direct replacement for the criminal charges, evidence and proof before a jury of one's peers that people in our country had come to expect for 790 years.

In May 2005, not long after the passing of the Control Order Bill, came New Labour's third general election victory, declining popularity and the Iraq War notwithstanding. Despite continuing battles with him over liberty and privacy in particular, I was glad to see Mr Clarke keep the Home Office brief. A consummate democrat, he always 'played the ball' rather than the woman, even to the point of meeting with Liberty regularly and telephoning with prior notice of controversial announcements that he knew we would oppose. We could, had and would do worse.

And when the 7/7 London bombings followed two months later, he chose the contemplative rather than the knee-jerk approach. The same, sadly, could not be said for the Prime Minister.

On 7 July 2005, a day after London won its bid to host the 2012 Olympics with a pitch based on its open multicultural values and internationalism, four young men – men as British as I – detonated bombs across central London, three on London Underground trains and the fourth on a red double-decker bus, killing themselves and fifty-two innocents in the process. When in due course their pictures were published, I recognized one of the victims: Karolina Gluck, a friendly receptionist who had greeted me when I went to speak at a Central London college a short time before.

I'll never forget that morning: coming into work and hearing news about some kind of 'disruption', 'perhaps electrical', on the Underground. The authorities were clearly keen not to cause widespread panic and it was a while before the real story emerged. I felt sick at the loss of life and optimism and at the even tougher times to come for Liberty. Completely irrationally, I phoned and phoned my son's nursery, even though it was just a short walk from Liberty's office and nowhere near the bombings. When the line was constantly engaged for a few minutes – what felt like an eternity – I told my senior colleagues that we should assemble the entire staff in an hour.

Then I ran over to the nursery and stole a glimpse of my three-year-old playing happily with his friends, before rushing back to the office to speak to my shaken colleagues – all of whom, thankfully, were safe. We spoke about how we felt and the personal and emotional attacks we might expect individually and institutionally in the times ahead, as the shock and grief of a capital and country turned to anger. (In truth, there was far less hatred directed at my Liberty colleagues than I had expected.) The rest of the day was oddly quiet and I spent it following the unfolding news of the atrocity. The next day, the reaction began.

My first duty was to appear on a breakfast television sofa next to my friend Melanie Phillips, with whom I had so often sparred on home affairs issues. She greeted me in the wings of the studio with a warm whisper – 'Are you and yours OK?' – before we went on to the set for a predictable conversation about closing the borders and locking down the country. I remember imploring the presenter to wait for more facts to emerge. How did we know that the murderers weren't British nationals?

And so it proved: the perpetrators were home-grown 'clean skins' who couldn't have been prevented by Belmarsh internment or control orders. Further they deliberately, it seems, carried identifying documents among their possessions – a detail which rendered the whole debate about identity cards irrelevant in this context. This didn't prevent some less statesmanlike politicians publicly blaming civil libertarians for the atrocity, but they were few in number and out of step with the prevailing mood of calm unity. The Home Secretary was more in tune. The day after the atrocity Charles Clarke resisted any temptation to make political capital out of the tragedy, speaking of the importance of civil liberties and conceding that identity cards would not have prevented the previous day's horrors.

In the days that followed, London's Mayor Ken Livingstone convened a memorial gathering in Trafalgar Square. There were many political speeches, calls for unity and liberal democracy and against knee-jerk prejudice. I read an elegiac passage from Peter Ackroyd's *London: The Biography*.

Although a failed second attack a couple of weeks later seemed unable to shake the general air of calm resolve, things were about to change. On 5 August, Prime Minister Blair convened a press conference at which he issued a now infamous statement: 'Let no one be in any doubt. The rules of the game are changing.' The 'game' was his national security policy and the 'rules' our fundamental rights and freedoms; the metaphor – in poor taste – summed up a speech whose emotional extravagance masked its tactical awareness. Blair had seized the moment. Deportation to places of torture was now back on the agenda, as was a new speech offence of 'condoning, glorifying or justifying terrorism'. Extreme but non-violent Islamist groups (Hizb ut-Tahrir) would be banned, as they were in parts of the Middle East. Suspects might be detained for up to six months without charge. In response to a placed question from a friendly journalist, Blair responded to Lord Hoffmann's famous flourish about the 'real threat to the life of the nation' with an 'I told you so' moment: Blair retorted that he doubted that those words would be uttered now – even though none of his mooted measures, let alone the one previously impugned by the Law Lords, would have prevented 7/7. This was nasty politics, pure and simple.

And while not six months but only three, in a fresh echo of apartheid, the ninety-day pre-charge detention policy was born and the Prime Minister's namesake, the Met Commissioner Sir Ian Blair, was employed as a cheerleader-in-chief for Number 10 policy. Policing and the police service would become politicized as never before, to the regret of many officers of all ranks. Many of them would stop me in the street in the months and years that followed to voice their support of and solidarity with Liberty's defence of the rule of law and the non-political, if imperfect, institution that they had chosen to serve.

But it wasn't all one way. A 7/7 survivor called Rachel North began blogging and speaking about her experiences of horror and beyond. The human kindness and generosity in that God-forsaken Piccadilly line carriage; the Muslim woman who gave up her headscarf as a bandage and the way fellow survivors had held hands in the dark. An advertising executive, Rachel came to be one of the greatest voices for fundamental rights and freedoms during the War on Terror and it was life-enhancing to share various platforms with her in the years that followed.

When terrorists attack us, they try to divide us. They want a panicked reaction and a divisive draconian response. It plays into their propaganda machine and by deeming them our terrible enemies against whom we must wage war, we dignify and glorify their hateful cause.

But what I learned on July 7 2005 was that we are each other's best security. We are the guardians of each other's liberties. I learned this when the bomb exploded and on each carriage of the train, trapped underground in the terrifying darkness and screaming women and men took each other's hands and comforted and calmed each other, shared water and passed around tissues, while other women and men ran to rescue the injured. Further horror and injury was prevented by people's calm and altruistic response. And in the darkness, you could not know if the person who reached to touch you was female or male or what race or religion they were. Just a stranger in the dark on whom your sanity and survival depended. I have held on to that lesson ever since.*

The battle for ninety days pre-charge detention was unedifying. Conducted by the government for political advantage – 'tough on terror' policies being seen as vote-winners – rather than real operational benefit, it wrecked the previous unity in the face of the threat and set democrats against each other in a war of words and values. Senior police officers, complete with uniform, were despatched to the Palace of Westminster to persuade wavering Labour backbenchers to vote for the measure and, while the eventual stage-managed compromise amendment was for twenty-eight days rather than three months, the 'game' was far from over. The prospect of even longer periods of police detention without charge or trial would loom for years to come.

It may be the recovering lawyer in me (or perhaps I'm only in remission), but I've always been infuriated by the way in which some people use the words 'charge' and 'trial' almost interchangeably in the context of detention. In our traditional Common Law legal system, one should be arrested on reason-

* Rachel North, *Guardian*, 11 July 2008

able suspicion, charged with evidence and convicted only when the incriminating case is proved beyond reasonable doubt.

We understand that complex conspiracies and international terrorism, in particular, are convoluted in their preparation and no doubt involve equal or greater care and complexity in the context of proving them before a jury. But the moment of charge is the moment that you know the offence of which you are accused. Under the ordinary law of the land and in other cases, involving murder and rape for example, it only takes hours or, at the outside, a few days – before you are formally accused or charged with the particulars of an offence. After this, you may or may not be granted bail. It may then be some months before the opportunity comes to have your day in court and defend yourself in front of a jury of your peers.

Lives are no doubt blighted by such an experience, but have you ever seen someone actually complain at the door of the Old Bailey when eventually acquitted? I suspect not. Instead, routinely flanked by their stalwart solicitor (we all love lawyers when we need them), family, friends and supporters, they deliver emotional speeches of varying eloquence about how they always knew that the truth would out and justice would be done.

Lengthy detention without charge – or 'internment' as it is properly called – is different. Here a person is effectively 'disappeared' without warning. It is the stuff of nightmares. Imagine the 5 a.m. knock on your front door: you are then taken from your life, work and loved ones on suspicion of some sort of terrorist activity – but you don't really know, because you're never properly told why you've been taken. In a short time, your life can change irretrievably. During your period of internment you can lose your job, relatives might die and children be born or go through some of those pivotal developmental moments that will never come again and which you will never experience with them. At the end of this indeterminate period, the authorities might decide that they have the wrong James

Brown, Shami Chakrabarti or Mohammad Khan. You may be let go with no more ceremony than that with which you were taken, your original clothes given to you in a plastic bag. No court door speech for you. No public vindication. Just the feeling of profound injustice festering in your heart and the hearts of those around you, who weren't originally attracted to terrorism as a means of effecting political change but who may now feel a little more persuaded. This is why lengthy pre-charge detention is as counterproductive as it is wrong, and is a measure traditionally rooted in countries from which so much terrorism has spread.

Try telling all this to prime ministers worried about appearing 'soft on terrorism' – whether the charge of softness is real or imagined, and whether it comes from a genuine public debate on national security or the private insecurities and demons with which we all live. The twenty-eight-day detention power was on the statute book by 2006 and by then New Labour infighting raged and speculation about prime ministerial transition was a public sport. Number 11 Downing Street was not just the residence of Her Majesty's Chancellor of the Exchequer, but a rival court: a government in waiting.

Emissaries from Number 11 were sent out to 'civil society' to develop 'new' New Labour thinking but also, no doubt, to commission allies for the transition to the next premiership. In the course of the year I lost count of the number of times that a minister or MP with nothing to do with the Home Office or Justice brief, but obviously associated with the Chancellor and aspiring Prime Minister Gordon Brown, wanted to have lunch or a drink and reassure me that 'it would all be different' when Mr Brown came to power. But there were early warnings, too. They came in the form of insights from insiders and even the odd speech from the Prime Minister-in-waiting, suggesting that things wouldn't be quite as different on identity cards and punishment without charge as others promised and I inevitably hoped.

When Blair finally resigned in the summer of 2007, Gordon Brown's assumption of the premiership was accompanied by new terror plots. In June there were two attempted terrorist attacks in London and Glasgow. There was a new Home Secretary, this time Jacqui Smith, the first woman ever to fill the role. Initially, the new Prime Minister bore the various horsemen of the apocalypse – widespread summer flooding, pestilence in the form of an outbreak of foot-and-mouth disease and terrorist attempts – with a statesman-like stoicism that warmed the heart. But autumn and the return of Parliament brought the true agenda. It was groundhog day: following the terrorist attempts, and wanting to be seen as sending out a signal of its strength and decisiveness, the new government was proving as obsessive about extended pre-charge detention as the old one had been.

This time there was lots of kind and polite 'engagement' from the prime minister's office: in late 2007 and 2008 I sometimes felt that I spent more time in Number 10 than in my own home or office. I was under the impression that I was being given the awesome burden and opportunity of persuading the Prime Minister that the new pre-charge detention limits under consideration – first fifty-six and then subsequently forty-two days – were unnecessary, counterproductive and wrong. No doubt, Brown and his colleagues felt that it was the other way round: that they had an opportunity to persuade me.

To be fair, I never felt completely 'played': during the early months of his government, Gordon Brown made some audible noises – sincere, no doubt – about constitutionalism and liberty. But when push came to shove, my colleagues and I felt as though we were having to fight the same intense battle again: trying to convince politicians, media and public alike that locking up suspects for six weeks or a thousand hours, without telling them why, would foster a greater sense of resentful victimhood – and, ultimately, lead to more potential terrorism – than it would ever prevent. Liberty's 'Charge or Release' campaign was born.

I remember meeting with senior colleagues for a day's strategy session and saying that this was a seminal moment for human rights in the United Kingdom and wider world. Lengthy pre-charge detention was a hallmark of tyrants: it was a symbolic issue around which all civil libertarians must coalesce or fragment irretrievably. The issue, in other words, was important in itself, but it also presented a line-in-the-sand moment for human rights more generally. What's more, if Britain were to take such a step in the face of the perennial threat posed by terrorism, what kind of example would it be setting for lesser, younger and putative democracies? Of course it was a risk for us to dedicate so much of our limited resources to this one issue – but we had no option, it was that important.

My close friend and colleague Liberty's long-time Legal Director James Welch had some typically wise words. 'I am afraid that we will put all our eggs in this basket, Shami. You know we might lose, and, if we do, I am worried about the impact on all of us and our organization. I am worried about the emotional effect on you.' It was kind, wise counsel indeed, but with comrades like him and values like ours, how could we possibly lose?

The government's significant signposting of the proposed measure meant that we, for once, had a little time to prepare. The Home Secretary announced the proposal in December 2007 – although we had been aware for some months that it was coming – and it would begin its journey through Parliament in 2008. Polling, fundraising and alternative policy development bolstered our effectiveness. We commissioned a poll which revealed that 54 per cent of the public believed the motivation for extending pre-charge detention was to look 'tough on terror' and only 13 per cent supported an extension to forty-two days, belying the assertion that the people of Britain will accept any measure if it is said to tackle terrorism. My colleague Sabina Frediani was the architect of the campaign and her private-sector marketing, sales and project management skills proved invaluable. One thing was clear: this campaign was far too important to contemplate simply winning the moral argument while the government got on with the business of enacting the legislation. The introduction of ninety-day pre-charge detention in one of the world's oldest democracies would only have been a victory for the terrorist. We were determined to win with our values, our rational arguments and the solidarity of minds and voices from across political and civil society.

Our position was straightforward. The new internment proposals were unnecessary, counterproductive and wrong. Unnecessary, because there were already a number of existing and potential policy measures that would better equip police and prosecutors in complex anti-terror investigations and trials than the proposed legislation. We think, for example, that it is madness that, blanket surveillance notwithstanding, material gained from intercepted telephone calls and emails is *not* admissible in a criminal trial in the UK. Wire-tap evidence is used to great effect almost everywhere else, including in the US, and while Liberty consistently calls for greater legal safeguards in its use – such as a judge signing a warrant, as she would do before your home or office is subject to physical search – we do not see the point of ever greater snooping if it cannot be proportionately and practically used in bringing criminals to justice. The argument against the admissibility of such evidence was never one about civil liberties. Instead, it stemmed from a time when the public at large was oblivious to the surveillance capability of the intelligence agencies more concerned with espionage against enemy governments (as in the Cold War) than traditional law enforcement. Thus inflexible cultures, kingdoms and mindsets develop that prevent the kind of innovation and cooperation that the various authorities so need in the face of evolving threats.

The new proposals were counterproductive. Interning in the name of 'freedom' people who then might turn out to be completely innocent is hardly the best advert for democratic values in a battle for hearts and minds.

And as for plain wrong – well, what can I say? You can be the judge. But before you pass sentence, look around the world at the company that you keep historically and geographically. International solidarity played an incredibly important part in this campaign. Early on, we commissioned lawyers to talk about the length and nature of pre-charge detention in their various jurisdictions. This was relatively straightforward in Common Law jurisdictions – such as Canada and Australia – where the moment of charge was as transparent as our own. As far as other legal systems were concerned – Civil Law jurisdictions such as France, Italy and Germany – we provided the various legal experts, whose credentials and advice we published in full, with a description of how our system works and the significance of the moment when an accused is told of the charge against them, in order that they can begin preparing their legal defence in earnest, even if this will take some time.

The results of this legal survey were astonishing and demonstrated just how out of touch the UK debate was with the rest of the democratic world. In Canada, the time limit for pre-charge detention was just twenty-four hours – a single day. Despite the continuing legal black hole for foreign nationals that is Guantanamo, in the US the criminal pre-charge detention limit was two days; in Russia, it was five and in France and Ireland, six and seven days respectively. So the UK's existing twenty-eight-day pre-charge detention period was already staggeringly disproportionate by international standards. The hard data made for a dramatic bar chart that, reproduced on billboards and in newspaper adverts, became the iconic image of Liberty's campaign.

It clearly shook the government: various apparatchiks were sent out to rubbish our research and even threatened a complaint to the Advertising Standards Authority. For my exhausted colleagues and me this provided a much needed moment of hilarity. Funnily enough, neither the complaint – nor an alternative international comparative analysis which might have been expected from a government that had pooh-poohed our findings and had embassies and high commissions all over the globe – was ever forthcoming.

There was another way in which the world came to the aid of our campaign. Human rights campaigners from across the globe voiced their solidarity and concern with what the United Kingdom government was proposing and the appalling example that, should the legislation pass, it would set for governments in their own homelands. Working with colleagues from Egypt, South Africa, the US, Hungary and elsewhere has been one of the most humbling and inspiring aspects of this work. Britain's might is no longer imperial or militaristic rule, but the soft power of rule of law values survives. If only our sometimes short-termist politicians could see it in front of their noses.

Liberty's campaign gathered momentum with media outlets, political pundits and civil society organizations as diverse as the trade union movement and the General Synod of the Church of England lending their voices in support. It was significant, we thought, that, despite London's particular history of terrorist attacks, all three major candidates in the 2008 mayoral election – Ken Livingstone, Boris Johnson and Brian Paddick – provided statements of solidarity with our campaign and against the government's proposal.

It was a bruising time. We were devoting so much energy to this fight and good news was thin on the ground. In addition to public advocacy, we began what one national newspaper called the 'Battle of the Tea Rooms'. At the time, opposition – Conservative and Liberal Democrat – policy was firmly against longer pre-charge detention, but as the political stakes rose,

Labour MPs would find it increasingly difficult to vote against the measure. Seeking to unite, rather than divide opinion across the political spectrum is never an easy proposition for human rights campaigners. My colleagues and I, desperately trying to gain a foothold within the Labour Party, sought one-to-one meetings with any Labour backbencher who would see us. In private, many were genuinely troubled by the policy, but hesitated to defy their party whips, who have a fearsome influence. Other backbenchers, trying to put a spoke in the wheels of our campaign, took up our offer of a meeting in order to waste valuable time as the crucial parliamentary votes loomed. The Home Secretary, herself a former whip, embarked on her own round of meetings as it became ever more obvious that the Chief Whip, Geoff Hoon, was promising much but delivering rather less in terms of rallying troops behind the increasingly unpopular policy. In a strange game of cabinet cross-dressing, Prime Minister Brown micro-managed the policy from Number 10 rather than the Home Secretary, who instead tried to whip the Labour Party into line. The not-so-loyal Chief Whip, anticipating a damaging defeat for the government, leaked stories to his own advantage in an attempt to come out of the crisis better than his senior colleagues.

A few short weeks before the crucial House of Commons vote in June 2008, our intelligence – based on direct discussions with those involved – indicated a Labour rebellion of sixty, more than enough to defeat the bill outright. At this point, the Prime Minister himself began to lobby to secure the vote. Subsequent newspaper stories recorded the offers made and deals done in an episode that does no credit to the Mother of Parliaments to achieve a nine-vote majority, equivalent to the number of Democratic Unionist Party MPs. This number was significant, the DUP having been in meetings with both major party leaders even as the debate in the main chamber raged on.

On 11 June 2008 I sat in the Strangers' Gallery – an area set aside in the Commons for the public to watch proceedings – despite being initially warned away by the office of the former Speaker Michael Martin. He got word to my colleagues earlier that afternoon that he didn't want 'Labour MPs to be distracted by visible presences' – presences who might no doubt stir their consciences. In the event I hotfooted it to Westminster and, when phoned by BBC Radio 4 presenter Martha Kearney, about to present the *World at One*, expressed my surprise at my own short-term ASBO designed to keep me away from the action. 'Tell the Speaker's office,' she replied, 'that you will either be preparing to take your place in the gallery this lunchtime or appearing on the radio to explain why not.' I took her advice and, on arrival at the Palace of Westminster, I found the gates of heaven strangely open.

Despite the tawdry behind-the-scenes wrangling, the debate itself was one of the best, with veteran Diane Abbott giving the speech of her life for which many plaudits and prizes rightly followed. The pressure on her was considerable. Although former Health Secretary Frank Dobson MP had assumed the role of chief rebel, with Abbott his loyal deputy, marshalling the rebels through the complex ins and outs of votes and amendments, the Speaker refused to call Frank. It fell to the MP for Hackney North and Stoke Newington to be the principal voice of the Labour Party's civil liberty conscience:

> I am a Londoner and I heard the last major IRA bomb, at Canary Wharf, from my kitchen in east London. Like thousands of Londoners, I waited for the early-morning call that assured me that friends and family on their way to work and school had not been caught up in those bombings. I will not take lectures from ministers about not taking terrorism seriously.
>
> I do not believe, as ministers continue to insist, that there is some trade-off between our liberties and the safety of the realm. What makes us free is what makes us safe, and what makes us safe will make us free . . .

... Of course the people whose rights some of us are trying to defend are unpopular and suspect. But if we as a parliament cannot stand up on this issue, and if people from our different ethnic communities cannot come here and genuinely reflect their fears and concerns, what is parliament for?

The full speech is worth reading – more than once. The Shadow Home Secretary, David Davis, himself a veteran of the forty-two-day campaign, described it as one of the best he had ever heard in the House of Commons. And that's how it was that evening as the debate unfolded: left and right united around democratic values. I sat in the Strangers' Gallery alongside law students and tourists, heart in my mouth, receiving periodic visits from MPs of different stripes in solidarity and hope. In the chamber below, it was like Grand Opera, government loyalists sidling up to potential rebels on the benches, sometimes in a pincer movement from either side. Then came the moment of voting; those around me wished me good luck. At what felt like the eleventh hour, the DUP stood up and went through to vote en masse – for the government. When the tellers announced the result, the DUP were greeted with scorn from the Conservative benches, who had united against forty-two days with only one exception in the form of Ann Widdecombe. Amid the cries of 'Judas' and 'thirty pieces of silver', I saw the Prime Minister give a little nod to the DUP leader before the uproar was quelled by the ever-dutiful Speaker Mr Martin. We had lost the Commons vote.

To this day a whiteboard – now framed – sits in Liberty House in Westminster showing the state of the parliamentary Labour Party as we understood it, twenty-four hours before the vote – when we had been, just, ahead. The board is titled 'The Battle for 42 Days'. It serves to remind us and, I hope, future generations of human rights campaigners of the value of committed, painstaking work – and that hope springs eternal.

*

For the story did not – does not – end there. The next day's newspapers were full of accounts of the dodgy deals and strong-arm tactics that the government had used to secure its vote. Later that day, David Davis announced that he was resigning his Yorkshire seat of Haltemprice and Howden to fight a by-election on the issue of forty-two days specifically and civil liberties in general, in protest at the way the government was playing fast and loose with hard-won freedoms.

Unsurprisingly, perhaps, Labour decided not to field a rival candidate: a surefire way to defuse Davis's campaign. For a while there was talk of the *Sun* newspaper putting up a candidate to make the authoritarian case, but this failed to materialize. Instead, 'sources close to the government' chose to attempt to discredit the former Shadow Home Secretary (replaced by Dominic Grieve QC MP) and our cause, with secret briefing to the media lobby that Davis was having an affair – with me. It was the lowest of political smears. I was as distressed for David's wife, my friend Doreen, as I was on my own behalf. It was a tough time, one of the toughest.

I have never experienced the adversity faced by human rights campaigners the world over who risk arrest and physical maltreatment at their governments' hands. I feel I've had a charmed life. Even after I've criticized senior ministers in print or national television, they've, for the most part, been ready to give me the time of day and sometimes a drink. But there was something about being personally briefed against by politicians in a way I believe would never have happened to a man, that made me feel very vulnerable and even jaded. Mercifully, however, the support of friends, colleagues and so many women in politics and the media, in particular, turned my spirits around before too long.

The moral and logical argument having been won, on 11 July David Davis won his by-election resoundingly and hosted a festival of liberty in his constituency in which a number of great campaigners participated. In the autumn of 2008 the bill returned to the House of Lords.

The House of Lords is a curious place. Its existence is difficult to justify to democrats from almost anywhere else in the world. How can you argue for a legislative model in which those who have inherited or been appointed to power, but not voted in, sit in a legislative chamber, even if it is invested with the ability only to scrutinize and delay rather than to make law?

I agree that if there were a nuclear holocaust or revolution, we would not design a new constitution in the way that ours has evolved. We would probably draw up a written constitution – in the manner of the US or France or South Africa – with a genuine separation of powers, in which the executive and legislative branches of the state are elected and the judicial branch is independent, or as independent from politics as one can imagine or contrive. But, make no mistake, such a model has its problems too, not least for the power that is inevitably invested in the highest or Supreme Court as the ultimate referees of the written constitution. Indeed, British politicians who frequently and conveniently balk at our unelected judges in a system that ultimately preserves parliamentary sovereignty – though in practice, too often, a sovereignty of the executive or government, even in the face of gross violations of fundamental values – might occasionally reflect on the far greater powers that are given to judges under written constitutions and bills of rights almost everywhere else in the free world.

When I was a young undergraduate at the LSE, we were regularly set essay questions about the UK's unelected second chamber, and whether it was a good thing. In those days one word would probably have done: 'No' – or, for better grades, 'Hell, no.' But I have to say that my last two decades of work at the heart of the UK constitution – both from the inside and the outside – have given me pause for thought. It seems to me now that democracy, like any other piece of fine-tuned machinery, must have both fixed and moving parts. The moving parts are of course the elected components that represent the heat and light of politics, which most people understand as the animating features in democratic life and rightly so. But the fixed components – usually in the form of independent referees or judges of 'the rules of the game' – are necessary too. In fact, in the absence of a written constitution and a Supreme Court with strike-down powers, they are vital. In our system, senior independent judges who possess only moral authority are complemented by the independent examiners of legislation in the upper chamber. In the end, the Lords too have only delaying powers, by virtue of the Parliament Acts, and moral authority but, in a climate of fear and feverish party politics, such delay – and with it the possibility of calm, rational debate – can be important and enough to persuade the elected components of our constitution to think again. And this was precisely what happened with the forty-two-days bill.

In the second chamber, the party whips have less sting, and the mood of the Labour Party suggested that the government was going to struggle much more this time. A narrow defeat for the bill in the Lords might have been expected, but the government could easily reverse such a setback – as is typical – when the bill returned to the Commons. A major drubbing in the Lords, however, would present the government's internment policy with a rather greater political challenge. And the government knew it. Once more government voices were out in force, including the Home Office minister Admiral Lord West, who once described himself as a 'simple sailor', when seeming less than completely fulsome in his support for the policy.

Former 'securocrats', many of them now on the cross benches of the Lords (the non-party political expert seats that are another point in the second chamber's favour), were obviously crucial mouthpieces for the government's argument. The very recently retired MI5 chief Baroness Eliza Manningham-Buller had been in the Lords a matter of days. In the end her early-evening speech – her first in the Lords – was as important as Diane Abbott's had been in the Commons. The government, clearly, had hoped for a crucial intervention from Baroness Manningham-Buller. It did not anticipate the form her intervention would take.

Thanking the second chamber for its warm welcome, the Baroness admitted that she would have liked more time to settle in and learn how things were done before 'opening my mouth', as she put it. However, she continued, she had already picked up one convention, 'which has been drummed home to me', which is that maiden speeches were to be short and non-controversial. 'I can do short,' she said,

but non-controversial is a bit trickier in the circumstances.

Since 9/11, we have had a great deal of terrorism legislation. One point that has not been made so far is that successful counter-terrorism work depends on a number of things, but in particular on good intelligence and good police work, not necessarily on changes in the law. That said, all the legislation has had some important and enabling provisions.

I applaud the fact that we are discussing now, rather than against the background of an atrocity, where this country wants to draw the line on issues such as pre-charge detention. I have considerable sympathy with the police on the collection of evidence which is very challenging given the need to move early, the amount of seized data, the complexity of cases and the forensics. I congratulate the anti-terrorist branch of the Metropolitan Police for the superb job it does. But arguments can be made to justify any time of detention, just as in other countries, although mercifully not here, they can be made to justify any method of interrogation.

In deciding what I believe on these matters, I have weighed up the balance between the right to life – the most important civil liberty – the fact that there is no such thing as complete security and the importance of our hard-won civil liberties. Therefore, on a matter of principle, I cannot support the proposal in the Bill for pre-charge detention of 42 days.

I understand that there are different views and that these judgments are honestly reached by others. I respect those views, but I do not see on a practical basis or on a principled one that these proposals are in any way workable for the reasons already mentioned and because of the need for the suspect to be given the right to a fair trial.

Finally, I have been fortunate in my career to have dealt with national security. It has been a great privilege. Our legislation covering the Security Service refers to the protection of parliamentary democracy. I have a plea: handling national security should, as far as possible, be above party politics, as it has been for most of my career. Faced by a severe terrorist threat, we should aim to reach, after debate and discussion, a broad, cross-party consensus on the way ahead. Polarized positions are damaging to what we are all trying to achieve in preventing – I underline that – detecting and countering terrorism.

There were audible gasps in the chamber, where once more I had the privilege of witnessing such important events. The Baroness's speech had a decisive impact. On 13 October 2008 peers finally voted the bill down by 309 votes to 118 – a majority of 191. The government, no doubt distracted by the practical and presentational priority of collapsing international markets, dropped the forty-two-day detention policy without much further ceremony. It had been a long battle – a hard and at times dirty battle. But the euphoria of defeating this odious policy has not diminished to this day.

When, following the 2010 general election, the Conservatives and Liberal Democrats took power in a coalition, civil liberties were supposedly the noble glue with which to bind a parliamentary marriage cobbled out of parliamentary arithmetic and still-failing markets. It was not to be. Punishment without charge in the form of control orders was sadly and rather shockingly rebranded in 2012 as Terrorism Prevention and Investigation Measures (TPIMs). Pre-charge detention, no doubt having achieved a better publicly understood and iconic status, was reduced to fourteen days (that's 336 hours or over 20,000 minutes) in a police cell without the suspect knowing why.

4

'Asbomania' and 'The Children of the Poor'

Don't knock ASBOs, it's the only qualification some of these kids will ever get.

– Linda Smith

We must not confuse dissent with disloyalty. We must remember always that accusation is not proof and that conviction depends upon evidence and due process of law. We will not walk in fear, one of another. We will not be driven by fear into an age of unreason if we dig deep in our history and our doctrine and remember that we are not descended from fearful men – not from men who feared to write, to associate, to speak and to defend the causes that were for the moment unpopular. Good night and good luck.

– Ed Murrow

By 2006 it sometimes felt as if our country had become an 'Asboland', where irritation, offence and nuisance were to be conflated with serious criminal behaviour and even, at times, terrorism. Prime Minister Tony Blair had given a number of speeches since his 1997 election win, most notably at Labour's 2005 party conference, boasting of his 'battering' of the criminal justice system to change. He suggested that anti-social behaviour, drug dealing, binge drinking and organized crime were 'twenty-first century' problems that couldn't be dealt with in a 'Dickensian', 'nineteenth-century' criminal justice system, which had at its heart the presumption of innocence. Blair was as bold and explicit in his attack on this 'golden thread' of the system as he was actually or theatrically naive as to the existence of all the social problems mentioned in earlier centuries. In 2004, he had remarked that 'the concern of a nineteenth-century criminal justice system was too many of the innocent being convicted'. His twenty-first-century concern, by contrast, focused on too many of the guilty going free.

The shallower roots of Blair's thinking lay in the 1990s, when Michael Howard, Home Secretary in John Major's Conservative government, had tempted the young Shadow Home Secretary (Tony Blair's most important job before becoming Labour leader in 1994) into a criminal justice-bashing arms race from which the UK has yet to escape. It is ironic that Howard and Blair, both previously able and successful lawyers, should turn on their own education and profession to denigrate the law, lawyers, legal aid – once such a proud pillar of the post-war welfare state – and even the judiciary, in a populist attempt to force crime and home affairs stories on to the front pages. This was a tactic designed to distract the electorate from the real issues: difficult and often expensive problems of inequality, parenting, education, substance abuse and mental health that riddled families and communities across classes and the land.

New Labour's repositioning on law and order was a result of the party's exasperation with 'Old' Labour being labelled 'soft' on crime. This was understandable not least because, as former Home Office minister Hazel Blears once pointed out to me, it is the poor who suffer most from crime and nuisance. Tony Blair's slogan 'Tough on crime, tough on the causes of crime', coined in 1995 when Labour was in opposition, was campaigning genius. But nearly a decade into its practical implementation, it translated into toughness on criminal justice and vulnerable people rather than on crime or its causes. I am conscious as I write this that many will find my liberal legal bleating predictable and imagine it to be based on a romantic lawyer's notion of courtroom procedure as some kind of elegant ballet, prioritizing justice for the individual over that for society as a whole. But this is not my prime concern.

The Central Criminal Court, better known as the Old Bailey, was erected in 1907 on the site of the infamous Newgate Prison. Above its entrance you can still read the inscription 'Defend the children of the poor and punish the wrongdoer'. The way that modern politics has so often pitted natural justice (as in fairness to individual defendants) and social justice (as in justice for the greater good) against each other has made me think long and hard about this famous phrase. Who exactly are the 'children of the poor' who must be defended? You might take the view that as these 'children' are pitted against the 'wrongdoer', the reference is only to victims of crime. That might sit well enough with the sword in Lady Justice's right hand, but not with the scales in her left. Alternatively, one could equate the exhortation to 'defend' literally, with the importance solely of defendants' rights. But that would surely warrant the use of the word 'but', instead of 'and', before the notion of punishing the wrongdoer.

It seems the message is both subtler and more realistic than that. The 'children of the poor' are everywhere. They are among all actual and potential victims and the accused.

This was always my biggest beef with the anti-social behaviour agenda. Dispensing with the presumption of innocence was premised on the idea that there was no need for it. As Prime Minister Blair once told the *Sun* newspaper: 'I can't physically come on to your street and stop the anti-social behaviour. But I can give the police the powers to do it. They know who the troublemakers are.'

Perhaps this premise was based on the belief that the police possess superhuman powers of deduction. More likely, in my view, it was the notion that separating the worthy from the unworthy 'poor' was just so blindingly obvious that there was no need to worry with centuries' worth of forensic and fair-trial protections for those suspected and accused of wrongdoing.

The government media machine presented a strange and depressing view of people in our country. On every housing estate in the land there were, it seemed, two hermetically sealed categories of humanity. In house number 1 you might find a 'decent, hard-working family'. Not wealthy perhaps, but doing their aspirational best – the 'right thing' – untroubled by emotional or mental problems, family breakdown, unemployment or substance abuse. This family was portrayed as almost Stepfordesque in its perfection. Next door you would find 'the neighbours from hell', suffering from and no doubt causing every kind of social problem imaginable. At one point the government mooted to move such people to 'sin bins' at the edge of towns. It was as astonishing as it was unrealistic.

Can any of us really claim that people are all so easily pigeon-holed? Aren't all people, and young people in particular, whether on council or country estates, in fact capable of being victims or suspects – guilty or otherwise of crime – in a single lunchtime, let alone a lifetime? The lazy populism of labelling and dividing people can appear comforting at first, but the comfort is ultimately short-term and illusory.

One of the many consequences of prioritizing policing and punishment over traditional social policy levers such as education, health and social work is that more and more people may be scooped up and shunted into a system that is so expensive in its human and financial costs that it really ought to be one of last resort.

Any police officer can walk down a busy high street and spot evidence of actual or potential crime, from regulatory and minor matters such as littering and car parking offences to rather more serious concerns. He or she judges how best to use their time and energies to prioritize what in their view requires attention. There are so many criminal offences on the statute book that this might be a harder task than you imagine, but once we blur and broaden the law into the world of anti-social behaviour, one that sits on the border between legality and illegality, things become trickier.

The original 1998 definition of 'anti-social behaviour' was 'behaviour likely to cause harassment, alarm or distress'. When asked by a television interviewer to clarify this definition, the formidable Hazel Blears replied: 'It means whatever the victim says it means.'

Think about how broad that definition and Blears's qualification are. A guest arrives late and inebriated to dinner. He smokes incessantly at the table without permission while other diners look plainly uncomfortable. He goes on to hog the conversation with bad and bawdy jokes. Later he makes an unwelcomed lunge for his hostess and, when challenged, punches his host. This is all anti-social behaviour in the colloquial sense – but exactly how much of it should be regulated by law, let alone the criminal code? Granted, our unpleasant guest has behaved in a pretty impolite fashion from the start, but if we censor for style and legislate for common courtesy, what have human beings left to give each other of their own free will? Isn't there a real danger of infantilizing all of us, with the idea that one should behave with consideration to others only for fear of punitive sanction?

The other problem is that some of us are very easily distressed. We are distressed by the mentally ill person who mutters strangely in the supermarket and the pair of boisterous youths laughing loudly on the bus, joking in a foreign language we don't understand. We are distressed by visible signs of misery, including those who find themselves begging on our streets – former servicemen and women from two long and bloody wars among them (ex-service personnel account for one in ten rough sleepers). Young people are rowdy, whether after the fine wine of Oxbridge dinners or after a couple of cans of cider in the town centre on a Saturday night. The 'children of the poor', however, have of course been more usual ASBO fodder. The majority of ASBOs were imposed in some of the poorest areas in the country.

In addition to incredibly vague and broad definitions of offending behaviour, this new mutant criminal law attempted to cheat the traditional system by altering the process and standard of proof. The legislation provided for the civil rather than the criminal test ('balance of probabilities' rather than 'beyond reasonable doubt'). The courts did their best to interpret this as a very high civil threshold but, when coupled with the admissibility of hearsay evidence ('it means whatever the victim says it means'), in practice it was almost unheard of for an ASBO application not to be granted. Of the 3,069 applications made in England and Wales between April and June 2009 only forty-two (or just over 1 per cent) were refused. But the government was disappointed with the relatively small number of applications by sceptical professionals and so employed a great deal of civil service energy in instigating wider use.

Another issue was the breadth of the conditions that could be placed on the ASBO. People were banned from walking down a particular side of a particular street; sometimes, they were barred from routes leading to their own homes or to the homes of close relatives. Some were banned from being sarcastic to their neighbours or wearing baseball caps. A suicidal woman was banned from bridges – an exquisite example of a pointlessly punitive solution to more complex problems. These and many other instances like them led to a high breach rate as people – youngsters in particular – had conditions imposed on them that they could never hope to meet and were thus set up to fail. But for the wider communities in which the offenders lived, ASBOs were fools' gold. Conditions often included banning people from certain areas, succeeding only in moving problems from one part of town to another, instead of proper prosecution and punishment of serious crime, or attempts to get to the root causes of more petty crimes and nuisances.

What was more, these orders created a personal criminal code for an individual who could wear the ASBO tag with a feeling of victimhood and persecution (always dangerous) or, worse still, as a badge of pride – a statement of their criminal credentials. Mr Blair once embellished a speech with an off-the-cuff anecdote from the election campaign trail. He had apparently stopped a young man to ask for his vote, only to be told that this was impossible as his ASBO barred him from the school that served as his polling station. The story brought gentle giggles and its intention was no doubt to add charm to a firm diatribe on serious matters. I found it positively chilling.

From a punitive summary justice point of view, the beauty of the ASBO process is the ability to catch the offender for walking on the cracks in the pavement without ever having to prove to the proper criminal standard the original sin of criminal damage or threats or real criminal behaviour. But instead of providing a last chance for people to stay out of the criminal justice system, as was suggested, it is instead the opposite: an often extremely unfair shortcut into punishment. And as breach of an ASBO is a criminal offence, even into our already over-stuffed prisons.

For good measure, and no doubt to have any hope of enforcement, many ASBOs had to be accompanied by substantial local publicity. There is no point in banning Mr X from the town centre unless those who might spot him are aware of the restrictions on his movements. But publicity or even 'naming and shaming', as it often came to be called – a phrase which for me evokes medieval stocks – brings with it the very real risk of stigma and vigilantism. One local authority ASBO project even provided CCTV feed into some residents' homes so that they could better keep an eye on their neighbourhood and their neighbours.

In 2009 there was the chief constable in a northern city

who used public money for hoardings in the major railway station showing well-known local criminals 'growing old in prison'. I accept that these were serious convicted criminals and not mere anti-social youngsters – but they were already in prison rather than on the run so the exercise was one of pure populist public relations. Further, when Liberty wrote to the police on behalf of older and child relatives who lacked the secure 'protection' of the prison estate and were subject to frightening vilification in their local community, our complaint miraculously appeared in regional and national newspapers with flattering macho depictions of the chief and the accusation that Liberty was fixated with the privacy of the convicted gangsters. This was also the period that gave us offenders performing community service wearing distinctive bright orange uniforms. First the stocks and then the chain gang, and all in the name of a so-called 'respect agenda'.

In July 2006, when he was no longer Home Secretary, the ever-energetic Blunkett challenged me to leave what he saw as my metropolitan liberal enclave (though South Londoners might think differently) to investigate and debate the value of ASBO-type legislation in his own parliamentary constituency in Sheffield. The encounter would be marshalled and recorded by Radio 4.

We went to a community centre on one of the more deprived estates in Blunkett's constituency. We sat at a large table with residents, mostly mums, who each introduced themselves by name and with an identical declaration of support for government policy. Almost 'AA style' they began: 'My name is X and I support the ASBOs.' Blunkett then introduced me, making a point that I was up from London and that people should be nice and polite to me. I felt completely set up for a fall, until the real conversation began.

It quickly became clear that the residents of the estate in question had been terrorized by a group of young men threatening them with machetes to have their way and create havoc.

My response was – and is – that this does not fall under the definition of anti-social behaviour but of serious violent crime. It's fair to say that people in more affluent areas of the country would not be satisfied with a civil 'stay away' injunction if they and their children experienced this kind of treatment. Nothing short of criminal prosecution for these men would and should do. It quickly dawned on my fellow mothers what I was trying to say: that these quick fixes are unfair to mistakenly suspected offenders, but they can also do terrible injustice to the victims of crime. Then one woman completely departed from the script. 'I have been a victim of crime,' she said, 'but I also have a son in the system.' At that point, she broke down. She needed no lectures from me or anyone else on the need for empathy with all of the 'children of the poor'.

When, in the summer of 2010, the new coalition government announced a review of the system of civil injunctions for anti-social behaviour, it seemed the ASBO, the Gangbo (injunctions designed to tackle gang related violence), the VOO (Violent Offender Order, intended to protect the public from an offender who is 'a current risk of inflicting serious harm') and the ever-expanding list of civil responses to behaviour ranging from the puerile to the seriously criminal were finally in the firing line. Sadly, Liberty's hopes were quickly dashed when, the following year, the Home Office revealed its intentions. While showcasing some alarming statistics about the failures of that whole regime, the consultation document, which eventually found expression in the Anti-Social Behaviour Crime and Policing Bill, lacked any kind of genuine new thinking on the subject. Preoccupied by the perceived bureaucracy, complexity and centralization of the system, together with the claim that penalties for breach were not tough enough, the Home Office was more concerned to streamline the process and to make the now inevitable noises about being seen to be tough on crime, rather than to tackle the fundamental issues surrounding ASBO-type legislation. Unsurprisingly, misdiagnosis led to bad medicine. The coalition government unveiled a simplified system containing fewer individual orders but framed to cover even wider categories of behaviour and activity. Another flurry of acronyms emerged: the Crimbo (Criminal Behaviour Order), the Public Space Protection Order or PSPO, issued in cases where 'activities carried on or likely to be carried on in a public place will have or have had a detrimental effect on the quality of life of those in the locality', and the IPNA (Injunction to Prevent Nuisance or Annoyance). The IPNA effectively replaced the ASBO. Now, sanctions could be imposed not just on anybody involved in activity perceived to be causing 'harassment, alarm and distress', but for any kind of behaviour seen to be causing 'nuisance and annoyance' – a full-spectrum definition if ever there was one.

Such a sweeping definition might feasibly allow an IPNA to be imposed on everyone from queue jumpers to noisy children, carol singers to trick-or-treaters. If I find an unthinking politician a 'nuisance and annoyance', should I be able to take out an ASBO against him? The coalition's great review of responses to anti-social behaviour had simply spawned a new generation of injunctions that were broader, easier to obtain, harder to comply with and carried harsher penalties than ever before. As the 2013 report of Parliament's influential Home Affairs Select Committee concluded, with more than a hint of exasperation:

> Each time successive Governments have amended the ASB regime, the definition of anti-social behaviour has grown wider, the standard of proof has fallen lower and the punishment for breach has toughened. This arms race must end. We are not convinced that widening the net to open up more kinds of behaviour to formal intervention will actually help to deal with the problem at hand.

In authoritarian times, it always seems to be the children who get the roughest end of the stick. For just as the so-called 'respect' agenda created a false distinction between the 'worthy' and 'unworthy' poor, it seemed to play into and exacerbate a deep-seated ambivalence towards the nation's young. We do so many things so well in the United Kingdom. For all our troubles, I would still for the most part rather be non-white here than in so many other countries that lack the richness and complexity of ethical, cultural and national differences that go back before the various imperial and post-imperial migrations of the nineteenth and twentieth centuries. Yet how many times have you heard someone from another continent or country point out Britain's strange, and at times still almost Victorian attitude towards its young? If my speech is free and yours expensive, the equation becomes even more fraught in the context of our own, as opposed to other people's children.

The concept of a 'spoilt child' conjures up the image of an object that can be treasured or 'spoilt' like a possession. We have a tendency to view our own kids as little angels who can do no wrong, while those of our neighbours are all too easily the 'hoodies' from hell. This tension in perception becomes even greater in a world of mobile communities and extended families and with an ageing population including many isolated older people, who can begin to see children and younger people as almost inherently threatening and for whom their own youth is a distant memory. People are always taken aback when I say that, at Liberty, we receive more angry correspondence for standing up for the rights of children than those of terror suspects. As if 'human rights' weren't frightening enough, the idea of children having rights is even more terrifying and challenging to our own communities, behaviours and responsibilities. If Eleanor Roosevelt was correct that rights begin in 'small places close to home', for some people at least, that is a little too close for comfort.

Professional teenager that I am now that I make a living out of saying 'that's not fair' to figures of authority, I feel anger on their behalf when I think of the legacy that my generation is in danger of leaving young people. They didn't crunch the credit or warm the planet. Nor did they start wars – real and metaphysical – at home and abroad. But their futures are precarious: they will most likely work longer and harder for less and with fewer benefits in order to support my generation into a longer and increasingly difficult old age.

It doesn't seem too much to ask that in relation to the young in particular, we try to understand what might lie behind disorderly behaviour. More important perhaps, that we try to ensure that young people's early encounters with the state might not come in the form of police officers. In addition to the near inevitability that general anti-social behaviour powers are disproportionately used against the young, two further toxic by-products of ASBO-style measures are worth highlighting: one a creature of the statute book and the other of technological ingenuity and commerce.

In addition to the power to arrest the young for suspected criminal behaviour, there have long been powers to remove young and vulnerable children to places of safety if they appear to be inappropriately at large in a way that puts them at risk. To this you can add offences and powers relating to compulsory school attendance and truancy. Indeed, in his pre-Home Office role as Education Secretary, the ASBO champion David Blunkett managed to make 'failing to secure' a child's school attendance an imprisonable offence. But where was the need for new legislation that allowed local authorities to effectively create a power to arrest and 'escort home' any under-sixteen-year-old found at large in the curfew zone between 9 p.m. and 6 a.m., even in the height of summer?

There was no need for suspicion that a young person was involved in anti-social behaviour even according to the broad and vague definition discussed earlier. The Anti-Social Behaviour Act of 2003 already provided local authorities with blanket powers that led to the creation of over 1,000 'dispersal zones' – designated areas where the police can, among other things, disperse groups of two or more people – in England and Wales between January 2004 and April 2006. How on earth did these powers provide children with a lesson in respect, let alone responsible behaviour, when they weren't even behaviour-related?

Back in 2005, Liberty successfully challenged the curfew measures by bringing a test case on behalf of 'W', a fifteen-year-old boy and 'model student' from the leafy London Borough of Richmond who was affected by a local curfew which would see unaccompanied under-sixteens forcibly removed to their homes if out between 9 p.m. and 6 a.m. With the aid of the interpretative power in section 3 of the Human Rights Act, the following year the Court of Appeal effectively emasculated the curfew measures by ruling that the police could only use force to remove children who were actually involved in or at risk from actual or imminently anticipated bad behaviour.

Six years later, however, things took a further and more explicit turn for the worse. In Tottenham on 4 August 2011, Mark Duggan was shot and killed by the Metropolitan Police, who believed him to be carrying a gun. Rioting followed throughout London and several other English cities. The unrest spread like wildfire in our modern world of twenty-four-hour news coverage and social media such as Facebook, Twitter and BlackBerry Messenger. This strife might have been avoided but for a completely incompetent and inadequate response to community concern from both the police and the Independent Police Complaints Commission. Liberty had campaigned for the creation of the IPCC, but it failed in speed and robustness in every major test of confidence, most significantly the shooting of Jean Charles de Menezes in July 2005. De Menezes was a Brazilian man killed by police at Stockwell tube station after he was misidentified as a terror suspect.

In 2011, an all-too-familiar debate ensued in the months that followed the riots. It felt like the harsh and divisive 1980s all over again. Some politicians and public figures called for more lethal weapons and political direction over the police instead of more understanding for the delicate relations between poor people and their police in our inner cities and the underlying causes of social unrest.

Some isolated voices suggested that the young and poor were not only or even primarily to blame for the riots of summer 2011. It was a right-of-centre journalist, the *Daily Mail* and *Telegraph* writer Peter Oborne, who put it best, pointing a finger at the rich and powerful for setting a bad example in the form of MPs' expenses, phone-hacking and a general lack of social awareness while wagging their authoritarian forefingers at the less fortunate: 'The culture of greed and impunity we are witnessing on our TV screens stretches right up into corporate boardrooms and the Cabinet. It embraces the police and large parts of our media. It is not just its damaged youth, but Britain itself that needs a moral reformation.'

Other responses were less reflective. Take the example of the London Borough of Wandsworth. One night in September 2011 I returned home from a speaking engagement and turned on the local news. A powerfully articulate Wandsworth resident was speaking of her imminent eviction by her local authority from council housing. Her near-adult son had been arrested for opportunistic looting during the riots and she was to be punished for it by being turfed on to the street.

Make no mistake, I understand how fragile the rule of law can be and how frightening its disappearance can be too. It is understandable that a minor theft during a riot might be punished more seriously than one in ordinary circumstances for fear of complete social breakdown otherwise ensuing. But that is surely no excuse for the double punishment of the poor?

Say that yours truly, a bourgeois liberal lawyer from South London, had come across an unsecured and unattended shop at the height of the riots. If I had been spotted helping myself to a bottle of wine from the already ransacked shelves and was arrested, I would no doubt be prosecuted for the crime. And were I found guilty, any subsequent sentence might be harsher than usual, in order to make an example of me. Arguably that makes sense, on account of my knowing better; on account of my privilege and quite possibly on account of my hypocrisy in daring to suggest how others should behave (not least on these pages) and in general as a human rights and rule of law campaigner. However, my prosecution and sentence would be once only and in the criminal courts to appropriate standards. Even if I went to prison, having served my term I would still be able to return to my private home (assuming that my mortgage was paid while I was inside). Why then should someone poorer, in social housing or private rental accommodation, suffer the double punishment of subsequent homelessness, not even for their own criminality but that of a family member or dependant? What if they are responsible for other family members – older parents or younger children, for instance – in addition to the errant teenager? What social objective is achieved by deliberately making people with problems homeless? I have rarely felt so impassioned as I did on watching the eloquent Maite de la Calva, a fervent Christian who had given considerable service to her community, taking on Wandsworth Council on the news. My late night email to Liberty staff insisting we help must have been met with exhausted groans by my long-suffering colleagues. Yet when I arrived at work at eight thirty the next morning my wonderful colleague the campaigning lawyer Emma Norton was already on the case.

After getting in touch with Maite we discovered she had been served with a Notice of Seeking Possession on 12 August 2011 stating she was likely to be in breach of her tenancy agreement and would be evicted if her son was convicted. Maite also has a young daughter, another innocent, wholly unconnected to her brother's crime, whom Wandsworth Council would also see punished. Some months later, even after the conviction of Maite's son, Wandsworth was persuaded by Liberty's public and legal campaign not to make Maite and her family homeless.

Ingenious discrimination is not the preserve only of politicians and policymakers. A Welsh scientist developed a device in 2005 that perfectly encapsulates arbitrary discrimination against children and young people. The 'mosquito' capitalizes on the fact that for most of us hearing deteriorates from our early twenties onwards, in the upper registers in particular. It is a device that emits a high-pitched noise capable of causing intense discomfort or even pain to younger ears. Completely unregulated from a public health point of view, it is available on the open market for shopkeepers and householders to attach to their property in order to disperse young people and stop them hanging around in the vicinity. If a young mother were regularly to push her pram past a particular shop, she might have no idea why her baby always screams at that point. At Liberty, we once bought a 'mosquito' in order to test out its effectiveness. I remember being completely oblivious to it (I was already in my early thirties). Then suddenly, one of our trainee solicitors covered her ears, burst into tears and ran out of the room in evident agony.

What kind of signal or lesson in respect, in the sense of fairness or mutuality of esteem, does this device provide to teenagers? Some women might take the view that men present a greater danger of nuisance or even violence on our streets than their female equivalents. But imagine if there were a physiological difference in hearing ranges: would this justify targeting men for such degrading treatment? And what if this kind of technology could be targeted against people of particular races? It doesn't bear thinking about and quite simply would not be allowed except in relation to our young whom we are charged – yes – with protecting, but also with nurturing, teaching and I would even dare suggest, respecting as well.

I'm hardly the first person to have raised these issues. Indeed,

one need only quote the maiden speech of a now senior politician who entered the House of Commons in 2005 and made
his parliamentary debut later that same May:

> The message that I received loud and clear in this campaign was
> that as we seek to revive our spirit of community, youth services
> must become a higher priority. What many young people on our
> streets told me is that there was nowhere for them to go and
> nothing for them to do. The young people whom I met are not
> yet cynical, nor are they without hope, nor are the vast majority
> troublemakers, but many feel that nobody really listens. They
> are tomorrow's voters – or regrettably, non-voters. Respect is a
> two-way street. Many older people feel that young people do
> not show enough respect, but young people feel neglected by
> our society.*

Ed Miliband ended his speech on a proud personal note. He
himself, he reminded the Commons, is the son of immigrants:
in his case, of a Jewish refugee from the Nazis who fled his
native Belgium for Britain in 1940.

The dilution of fairness and the creation of quick-fix mutant
ASBO justice belittles the serious suffering of victims and
sometimes creates extra ones in the form of miscarriages of
justice. It flirts with mob rule and is particularly tough on the
young. But in such an authoritarian climate, other democratic
dangers lurk. Protection from 'distress' quickly morphs into a
right 'not to be offended' and in a free society this is one right
that must never exist. If we are all so infantilized and thin-
skinned that we seek a right not to be irritated or offended,
what are the consequences for cogent political dissent?

It's no coincidence that the period of 'Asbomania' also saw
laws passed that banned people from protesting in Parliament
Square; peace protesters arrested and prosecuted for reading

* Ed Miliband MP, 23 May 2005

out the names of the war dead at the Cenotaph; young men arrested for wearing anti-monarchist T-shirts or for carrying placards suggesting that 'Scientology is a cult'; and schoolchildren 'kettled' like cattle for protesting against university tuition fees. 'Kettling', incidentally, allows police effectively to detain protesters when there is no suspicion of criminal behaviour.

Human rights law with its special protection for free speech and association has offered considerable defence against this authoritarian trend. But even this kind of constitutional or 'higher law' will remain a dead letter if the people it is designed to protect, in particular the poorest and most vulnerable, simply cannot afford or otherwise gain access to legal advice and representation. Indeed, the lack of free, independent and fearless lawyers is one reason why it has been possible for some of the most notorious tyrannies in world history to have laughably exquisite and faultless written constitutions which bear no resemblance at all to the day-to-day experience of the ordinary people living under them. So the rule of law can be overtly undermined not only by tampering with traditional legal process protection but also by effectively locking the courtroom door to all but the wealthiest and most powerful.

I grew up in a post-war Britain that prided itself on the welfare state. Apart from my parents, the greatest influence on me was the state education system, which shaped my life chances from toddlerhood to the age of twenty-two, when I left the LSE with a law degree and modest student debt. I never had to pay a tuition fee until I went to read for the bar as a post-graduate, and even that was a real struggle.

I'm also proud to have grown up in a country where, if you were knocked down by a car in the street as I once was, on the way to school, you would be scraped up by an ambulance and taken to the emergency room without anyone checking your purse or wallet for money or health insurance, but only to find out your name and contact details of loved ones. Politicians recognize all too well the pride that we all share in our NHS, which is presumably why they try to outdo each other in their declarations of devotion to it and portray any reforms they want to make to it as managerial and organizational rather than threatening and ideological. Some would argue that sentimental speeches are a sleight of hand that allows politicians to institute quite radical and fundamental changes to healthcare while putting on white coats in fantasy photo ops designed to make them look (or even perhaps feel) like Dr Ross or Dr Kildare.

But contrast the NHS with legal aid, another great pillar of the post-war settlement designed to benefit all of us. When I grew up, if you were poor and accused of a crime, or in legal difficulty related to your family, welfare, housing or debt, you could get access to free advice and representation. Such early advice is often crucial, before people's problems spiral out of control. But the most vulnerable have some of the most crucial power relationships in their lives with parts of the state. It was hardly surprising that the authoritarian politicians of the mid-90s and beyond would seek to undermine this important potential check on their power.

The same politicians that gave us the Human Rights Act began to denigrate the lawyers and legal services that were capable of implementing that legislation on behalf of ordinary people. Tony Blair – a trained barrister – made speeches attacking the 'gravy train' of legal aid. But the reality was that most lawyers involved in the provision of legal aid were paid less than NHS doctors – their medical equivalents – not to mention some of their college chums who went to the City to earn hefty multiples of their salary. Legal aid is a hard furrow to plough. Often, clients – ranging from suspects from the 'Asbolands' of the inner cities to the detainees of the War on Terror – prove to be difficult for many and complex reasons. It is another particular trick of authoritarian governments the world over to equate lawyers with the clients they represent as a means of undermining the importance of providing access to justice. It's worth remarking, however, that the lawyers who made fortunes advising the people and financial institutions that plunged the world into recession in 2008 rarely attracted the same political or media bile.

One devastating attack on legal aid was to restrict its availability to fewer and fewer people over time. I suppose that one of the reasons so many of us love the NHS and indeed that other national, if too easily tarnished treasure the BBC, is that we have all experienced its value to some degree or another. Even by the time the Human Rights Act was brought into force in 2000 civil legal aid was strictly means tested. It was becoming increasingly difficult to access unless you were almost completely destitute. Ownership of any assets – a home or a car, for example – would most likely disqualify you from receiving it. So going to court – for instance, to assert their privacy rights – was going to prove almost impossible for ordinary working people: the taxi driver, nursery worker and whole swathes of the population.

Meanwhile, movie stars received in-depth coverage for – quite rightly – defending their rights to a private life. Even the same media empires that campaign to trash human rights legislation would fight bitter legal battles over free expression. We would also of course read about the Act used as the last defence of the terror suspect and refugee and all the rancid populist political rhetoric that went with those high profile post-9/11 test cases.

Even if one of these 'decent hard-working law-abiding people' were able to gain access to free advice or legal representation, suing the authorities still brought with it the risk of having to pay the deep-pocketed defendant's costs in the event of losing. At the same time law centres were dying, so this kind of free service was barely able to scratch the surface of unmet need. Most people could never take on such a financial risk.

Because those of modest and moderate means have been squeezed out of the system many important test challenges to bad practice and abuses of power have not been brought. What's more, as legal aid practice became less financially sustainable and ever more of a bureaucratic nightmare, excellent firms went out of business. Tooks Chambers, who defended striking miners in the 1980s, took on miscarriages of justice such as the case of the Birmingham Six and represented Stephen Lawrence's family, dissolved in December 2013 as a direct result of legal aid cuts. Legal aid deserts began to appear in large parts of our small country so that people had to travel miles to find help – that is, if they still qualified for it.

As if New Labour's undermining of public sympathy for legal aid through spin, rhetoric and exclusion from protection weren't bad enough, things would get even worse under the coalition government. The Legal Aid Act 2012 removed whole groups, not just of so-called 'ordinary people', but now the very poorest in the land, from legal support in their times of greatest personal need. For most cases involving housing, welfare, medical negligence, employment, debt and immigration, financial support was no longer available. If you lost your job in the recession and were struggling to deal with debt there was now to be no help, practically until the point that you faced eviction – a cruel and counterproductive social policy if ever there was one, when a little good early professional advice might help people back on track, and be cheaper for the taxpayer too.

Under the same Act, legal advice and help on welfare law were no longer available, unless and until you exceptionally found yourself arguing some rarefied point of law in a higher tribunal. In practice and given the repeated evidence of bad decision-making at the Department for Work and Pensions, this means many children, disabled, poor and otherwise vulnerable people are not able to understand their benefits. People didn't get the financial support to which they were entitled in the worst recession in living memory.

In all but a handful of exceptional cases private family matters were largely removed from legal aid provision. The reason given for this was that mediation should be provided instead. So if Social Services take your son or daughter from you, you may qualify for legal aid. But if your ex-partner denies you any contact with your child and refuses to entertain mediation, no advice or representation is available.

And if it weren't bad enough that Parliament should pass a law to deny access to justice to the worst off in austerity Britain, the Act contains a power for the Lord Chancellor (who is also the Justice Secretary) to continue removing further areas of legal provision by 'secondary legislation', that is, legislation which is hardly scrutinized by Parliament at all. One of the first measures brought in by this all-too-common underhand legislative method was to impose a residency test on people seeking legal aid. Quite right too, you might think: why should the British taxpayer fund people abroad or newly arrived here to sue our government? But what about the torture victims of our military and security adventures overseas? If they had been excluded from our courts, how would we have known what was being done in our name? What about the women in immigration detention centres who allege sexual abuse by their male guards? We should never forget that 'public interest law' is so named for a reason: if the powerful can get away with flouting anyone's rights, in the end they will flout everyone's.

Predictably, prisoners were also excluded from legal aid should they want to challenge their treatment or conditions. Few will shed tears over such a measure but we should remember that, to the amazement of people all over the world, the age of criminal responsibility is only ten years old in this country. Young teenagers can find themselves in custody and subject to 'control and restraint' and other cruel treatment, treatment capable of causing serious injury and even death. Fifteen-year-old Gareth Myatt choked and died while being restrained by guards at Rainsbrook secure training centre. If you've ever had a child who has been in trouble, remember the mother who was David Blunkett's constituent during our ASBO debate in

Sheffield. The Prison Reform Trust informs us that 30 per cent of boys and 44 per cent of girls in custody have spent some time in care. One in eight of the children in custody has experienced the death of a parent or sibling, while 46 per cent of women prisoners have suffered domestic abuse. If it's really too hard to care about other people's children, remember the frailties and vulnerabilities of our own and where we go but for the grace of God or just plain good fortune.

Whatever they may have done or are accused of having done (many of those in custody are on remand awaiting trial) prisoners are some of the most vulnerable people in any society. As Winston Churchill famously said, our treatment of prisoners is one of the most important tests of our values as a society, '. . . the treatment of crime and criminals mark and measure the stored up strength of a nation, and are the sign and proof of a living virtue in it'.

In 2013 the coalition consulted the public on the compulsory competitive tendering of criminal defence work and the implementation of incentivized payment models that would create a conflict between the interests of a client and their lawyer. For instance, rewarding the professional for a guilty plea. There was talk of legal aid 'factories' to provide cut-price advice. This particular proposal was defeated in the short term. But for how long can we fight off these fundamental changes to the way law is administered in this country if we fail to grasp the importance of access to justice and true equality under the law for the vulnerable and the powerful, whether they be big business or the state itself?

As it is, the decreasing remuneration of criminal lawyers makes it more likely that in the future, as in the United States where they don't have either an NHS or a legal aid system, the legal fate of poor people facing the gravest criminal charges and consequences will be left in the hands of idealistic but inexperienced graduates straight out of law school.

Louise Christian is one of the most celebrated legal aid

lawyers of her generation, with clients ranging from terror suspects to the families of those killed in rail and other major disasters. She left a promising early career in a leading City law firm many years ago for a life of legal public service. This is how she sees the legal state we're in:

> The effective destruction of legal aid means that in many situations, poor people can no longer get redress for government wrongdoing in the civil courts and that they face getting a criminal conviction in the criminal courts because of substandard legal representation. It cannot be right that we can no longer afford equal access to justice in the 21st century.

Quite so.

5

No Torture, No Compromise? The Heart of Darkness, Secrets and Lies

Torture cannot be justified in any set of circumstances at all.

> – Tony Blair, 7 December 2005

Well it all depends on what you mean by rendition. If it is something that is unlawful I totally disapprove of it; if it is lawful, I don't disapprove of it.

> – Tony Blair, 22 December 2005

Let's face it – if you really think there are only fifty shades of grey, you probably need a bigger box of crayons. I've already discussed some of the many necessary ethical dilemmas confronting democrats who treasure fundamental human rights, especially in the face of challenges to law, order and national security. While we cherish our privacy, liberty, free expression and association rights among so many others, few of us would suggest that they can ever be completely absolute or unqualified. So we argue for any interference with these rights to be proportionate rather than counterproductive to the threats we seek to address. We demand tight and accessible legal process protections, especially for the application of a calm and even hand to ensure equal treatment and avoid the discrimination that divides us by fostering injustice and the natural resentment that follows.

Yet if human rights are to mean anything they must have hard edges as well as smooth corners. They must be robust as well as flexible. Some absolutes do exist. The rules against torture and slavery in particular. Since 9/11 many have questioned why this should be the case. I've lost count of the number of times people have asked me why it is that the Human Rights Convention allows killing – for example on the battlefield or even in peace time if strictly necessary to save life – but forbids inhuman and degrading treatment and torture in all circumstances, including emergencies such as war or a terrorist attack. From the routine way in which the scenario is trotted out to justify 'enhanced interrogation techniques', another classic War on Terror euphemism, you would think that ticking nuclear bombs are found every other day at tube stations all over the democratic world. Nonetheless, this depressing or even shocking, oft repeated question deserves a serious answer.

Remember how the modern notion of international human rights was born. The drafters of the Universal Declaration and the European Convention on Human Rights did not just witness the barbarity of conventional armed conflict during the Second World War, but saw images and heard testimony from survivors of Nazi concentration and extermination camps and Japanese prisoner-of-war camps. It is hardly surprising, therefore, that the concepts of torture, inhumanity and degradation were foremost in their minds. If that provides a historical context for the absolute rule against torture, what is the philosophical justification, especially if you are not a pacifist and are prepared to tolerate killing as a lawful and moral action in certain extreme circumstances?

Human rights instruments take life and death extremely seriously. The right to life in Article 2 of the Convention and Human Rights Act provides for lawful killing only when 'absolutely necessary' to protect life, prevent a prisoner escaping or quell a riot. The test of absolute necessity is deliberately tighter than the idea of 'proportionality' that we use when, for example, intruding on people's privacy and family life. Further, the obligation against the state isn't just a negative one as far as the lives of its people are concerned. It extends also to a positive duty to protect life and investigate suspicious deaths.

Yet the right to life is not absolute. The right not to be tortured or subjected to inhuman treatment, on the other hand, is.

I think perhaps the biggest clue lies in the word 'inhuman'. Large sections of the British population eat meat and some even hunt or rear animals for slaughter. However, I suspect that many or even most of this group, including large numbers who probably wouldn't remotely associate themselves with the idea of 'animal rights', disapprove of unnecessary cruelty, even to those animals that have been brought into the world for the sole purpose of human food consumption. Why is that? I think it is because of a fundamental understanding that torture and cruelty do something hideous, not just to the victim, but to the perpetrator and the wider society of which she is a part.

We don't all like to talk about it, but we will all die one day. In practical terms, an absolute 'right to life' would require medical miracles rather than philosophical or legal development. We can hope for long, happy and fulfilled lives but still death will come. Torture and degradation need not. To take another's life and choose the moment of their ending is quite literally to 'play God'. It is, rightly, almost always unacceptable. However, to inflict inhuman treatment is to play a yet more terrifying role, and in so doing to force a fellow human being to endure a darkness of which we should aspire to rid the world.

The last decade proved how far from that goal we still are. It also demonstrated how near to home some of the challenges and obstacles are. The contagion of outsourcing, excusing and sugar-coating torture began in the United States with Guantanamo, rendition, 'enhanced interrogation techniques' (EITs) and so-called 'black sites' around the world, including in Eastern Europe. Debates continue to rage about the reliability of intelligence gained by such methods. I have greater stores of moral than physical courage and an extremely low threshold for pain. The less than completely tender mercies of the natural childbirth lobby notwithstanding ('you're not a real woman unless you do it in the bushes with nothing but Mozart and aromatherapy oil for pain relief'), I only managed to give birth with a great deal of pharmaceutical and eventual surgical assistance. If you tortured me, I suspect that I would tell you whatever I thought you wanted to hear – whatever might make the excruciating pain cease. The other side of the argument is that the material can be reliable sometimes and could possibly therefore foil the plans of a particular terrorist group. Well, what sort of reliable is that?

David Davis puts the point starkly:

> Sheikh al-Libi was an al-Qaeda emir at the al-Khaldan training camp in Afghanistan. Captured by the Pakistanis, he proved a useful source when he was interrogated by the FBI using conventional methods. When the CIA took him over, however, they sent him to Egypt to be tortured to obtain more information. Under torture he 'confessed' that two al-Qaeda operatives were sent to Iraq for training in use of chemical and biological weapons, exactly what the Americans wanted to hear, and no doubt what was necessary to bring his suffering to an end. This was the evidence that Colin Powell was referring to when he told the UN he had 'proof' of Iraqi WMD to justify the war.
>
> It was, of course, not true. Sheikh al-Libi later recanted his confession, but not before hundreds of thousands of innocent Iraqis had died.
>
> The Egyptians were embarrassed. Sheikh al-Libi had been sent back to Libya to be imprisoned by Gadaffi. The Egyptian head of intelligence, Omar Suleiman, visited in 2009. Before he left, al-Libi had 'committed suicide' in his cell. You may draw your own conclusions.

It's like the ticking bomb tale turned on its head. The question often posed in this debate is whether you would torture someone for information if you knew there was a bomb about to go off. Except this wasn't an undergraduate hypothetical. It really happened.

If there is a special place in hell for the doctors who participated in torture by way of medical experiments in the darkest moments of the twentieth century, what about the lawyers who excused and legitimized torture with the thought experiments of the twenty-first? As late as January 2014, the former top CIA lawyer John Rizzo was promoting his aptly titled book *Company Man* with media appearances in which he justified torture techniques including sleep deprivation, cramped confinement, placing suspects in stress positions and waterboarding them. In an interview with Gordon Corera for BBC2's *Newsnight* programme Rizzo, the 'company man', admitted that he had reinterpreted the word 'torture' to suit his clients and that the justification was fear of another 9/11 rather than any obvious legal reasoning. In the follow-up studio debate that I had with the eminent retired Harvard law professor Alan Dershowitz, the once-renowned liberal lawyer argued that while he did not personally approve of torture, as it happens anyway it ought to be legalized and subject to signed 'warrants'. He made an analogy with the death penalty which, on reflection, seemed to reveal how the huge barbarism of that continuing practice in the United States can be used incrementally to justify everything from drone strikes and targeted assassinations to torture.

My own horror at the death penalty began my personal human rights journey. For this I have my father to thank. As an eleven-year-old girl watching the TV news in my parents' North West London semi I remember being transfixed by the seemingly endless updates in the hunt for the Yorkshire Ripper. One evening, especially unnerved by the coverage, I said something about what they should do to 'this animal' or 'monster', or something like that, when he was caught.

In my dad's first and perhaps last Atticus Finch moment, he

asked me to consider that no justice system capable of human design or operation can ever be perfect. What would it feel like, I remember him saying, to be the one wrongly convicted person in a thousand or million walking to the gallows or electric chair or lethal injection? What would it feel like when every due process appeal was exhausted and when even your own family no longer believed you – yet you went to your death knowing that you didn't do that terrible thing for which you were about to be executed?

That evening my father's words captured my imagination and turned my stomach and it makes the hairs on my neck stand up even today as I write. I duly reconsidered and never looked back. If I went on in adult life to become the bug-bear of so many authoritarian men, they only have one of their own number – my dear old dad – to blame.

But I suppose that if you believe in the death penalty and have it at the heart of your justice system it would seem reasonable to assassinate Osama bin Laden. He was after all the most obvious and notoriously 'guilty' man in the world, so putting him on trial before you execute him is surely just a bit of a circus and a dangerous one at that. This is what the War on Terror was capable of doing to lawyers. It could turn stupid ones into yes men for corner-cutting and cruelty and clever ones into the architects of increasingly byzantine processes with which to conceal or even legitimize barbarism.

By the beginning of 2009 the game was up on covering up the British government's complicity in torture. In early February I appeared on BBC1's *Question Time* programme with the Right Honourable Geoff Hoon MP (then Transport Secretary). Our heated exchange seemed to divide viewers along gender lines – at one point he conformed to stereotype by describing me as 'emotional'. This was his response to my profound disgust at the attempts of his government to cover up their antics in court, even to the point of telling senior judges to keep passages of legal decisions critical of the authorities a secret. This had come to a head in the case of Binyam Mohamed, an Ethiopian who had been resident in the United Kingdom but who, in 2002, was arrested in Pakistan and 'rendered' by the United States to Morocco where there was allegedly a CIA black site where he was tortured and interrogated for eighteen months.

It was proved that MI5 agents had participated in Mohamed's interrogation, despite knowing about his ill-treatment, which included extensive beatings, subjection to loud noise – sensory bombardment – for days on end, and scalpel cuts to his chest and genitals. MI5 agents also provided pictures and information from the UK for the interrogating agents to put to him, and received information gleaned from his interrogation in return. The idea was to get the suspect to confess to involvement in a dirty bomb plot against a US city. Though his torturers extracted a statement from him at the time, Mohamed subsequently retracted it and maintains his innocence of terrorism charges.

Subsequent civil proceedings against the UK government in London, initially to gain access to vital evidence of the torture, became incredibly important for a number of reasons. Firstly, they once more highlighted governments' capacity to contract out their dirty work, whether to fellow democratic governments, as in the 'special relationship' with the US, who treat each other's territories and nationals with less respect than their own, or even to less 'developed' allied nations, where grave human rights violations such as torture are routine and accepted. Democratic states that launder their torture are no better than the tyrannies they conspire with. And what precisely is the difference between rendering someone or deporting them to a place of torture? Only that in the case of rendition you have the express prior motive of extracting intelligence.

Even now, years after the heart of darkness that was rendition was laid bare, politicians remain hugely frustrated at their inability to deport foreign suspects to places of torture. This issue continues to be at the forefront of the human rights debate. The case of Abu Qatada, in particular, still haunts me like a stalker ex-boyfriend. Everywhere I go, the time that it took to get the ranty cleric and former Belmarsh detainee out of the country is put to me as a classic example of 'human rights madness'. Let's examine our sanity, humanity and logic a little more closely. There were umpteen offences with which he might have been charged, for example, incitement and soliciting murder. Instead he was subject to various forms of lengthy detention and subsequent community restriction without trial. The prize that successive governments sought was deportation rather than prosecution. Possibly they believed it would be the easier option. Ironically, while politicians can make up and change policy in the spur of a soundbite, the machinery of practical administration can be slow and reluctant to re-evaluate strategy, even after years of failure.

After some years of legal questions and challenges, about the safety of various Middle Eastern countries in particular, the government (originally New Labour) attempted to negotiate so-called 'Memoranda of Understanding'. These MOUs were basically designed to be gentlemen's agreements rather than legal commitments with those countries, Jordan included, in an attempt to extract promises not to torture those deported from the UK. The aim was to pacify and persuade UK and European Human Rights Courts that our government was adequately protecting those it was about to deport.

This approach was understandably controversial. If a country cannot be trusted – on the basis of, for example, credible reports from agencies such as the US State Department, UN monitoring bodies and Human Rights Watch – to respect international multilateral treaties and conventions against torture, why would its leaders be trusted to honour a convenient little bilateral deal stitched up for the convenience of a British Home Secretary trying to be shot of a high-profile undesirable? There was and is a real fear on the part of Liberty and others that these pacts aren't worth the paper they're written on. Also, an international human rights monitor of any integrity would surely refuse to police such a specific agreement. It's difficult to imagine who would volunteer to go and confirm the good health of a notorious suspect recently deported from Britain while listening to the screams of a torture victim in the next cell.

Nonetheless, there was a rare precedent for deals of this kind. The United States still executes people, often after lengthy periods on death row. This is anathema to European notions of common decency and human rights. For some years suspects or defendants facing capital charges in the US have been extradited there only on the basis of an understanding with our own government that the death penalty cannot apply. To date this seems to have been honoured.

Abu Qatada's most obvious return destination was Jordan, of which he was a citizen. For years the torture and fair trial record of this monarchy raged in our domestic courts as well as the Human Rights Court in Strasbourg. Eventually, however, coalition Conservative Home Secretary Theresa May announced in 2012 that she had secured not just a deal with Jordan in relation to this particular terror suspect's treatment but crucially, a change to its constitution banning the use of evidence obtained by torture. This development was obviously instrumental in Abu Qatada's eventual departure from Britain a year later. Theresa May could arguably have claimed a victory for human rights and the rule of law at home and abroad. Not only had she deported the suspect while respecting the previous findings of our courts, she had secured a change to the law of another country, way beyond the reach of the European Convention, that ought to make torture just a little less convenient or palatable in that jurisdiction. Sadly and perversely, in my view, she stole moral defeat from the jaws of victory and spoke instead of 'reforming' the Convention and perhaps pulling out of it altogether.

To return to Binyam Mohamed, his case also demonstrated how our government could hide behind the 'control principle', whereby intelligence shared with an ally is not revealed without the originator's permission, to conceal its own bad behaviour. In this instance, in 2009 government lawyers argued that paragraphs of the court judgment that criticized MI5 on account of its awareness of Binyam Mohamed's ill-treatment could not be made public because of the control principle. However, it also quickly emerged that the Foreign Office had conveniently not even bothered to ask permission of the relatively young Obama administration for the relevant material to be made public.

This highlighted the symbiotic but toxic relationship between secrecy and torture and the inordinate lengths that governments and securocrats will sometimes go to in the avoidance of scrutiny and accountability, whether to public opinion or even the law. When the judicial criticism of the government's attempt to suppress evidence was eventually published in February 2010, certain parts of the intelligence and political establishment were nothing short of furious and this indignation festered away until beyond the 2010 general election. It found eventual expression (some policies, practices and powerful personnel are unaffected by democratic elections) in the Justice and Security Act of 2013 – a piece of legislation which has absolutely nothing to do with either justice or security.

The Justice and Security Act replaces fair and even-handed civil trials in which a government, military, 'spook' or police party to litigation participates under the same rules as their opponent, with the 'closed material procedures' of the Special Immigration Commission that were used to perfume internment in Belmarsh and then punishment without charge under control orders and their replacement, TPIMs. Under this procedure, the ordinary person, usually someone making a civil claim in relation to some kind of alleged bad behaviour by the state, finds herself shut out of large parts of the proceedings, sometimes for several days of argument, while the lawyers on the other side get to present evidence and argument in secret to the presiding judge. Hardly equality before the law. Instead it's a bit like a football match where one side is repeatedly ordered off the field so that the other team can be alone with the referee on an empty pitch with an open goal. Successive governments have tried to argue that the presence of the judge operates as an adequate safeguard of justice. But how can that be? The judge doesn't know what the claimant would have argued if she were in the room and with sight of the case against her. The referee cannot substitute for the team that isn't even in the park.

Just as politicians can undermine the judiciary with dangerous, disrespectful rhetoric about unwelcome judgments and the unelected status of the judiciary, they can equally, and invidiously, undermine the rule of law by co-opting it and making it too cosy and complicit with administration in general and the secret state in particular. Why should a kid on a council estate respect a magistrate's order if a prime minister won't respect the highest courts in the land?

So much for the 'Justice' part of the Act's title. What about the 'Security' ambition? When, in the past, secret commissions were substituted for fair trial courts it was invariably in the name of some kind of practical security outcome. The original SIAC procedure aimed to remove foreign national terror suspects from the country. Belmarsh was about putting them in prison while control orders and TPIMs placed terror suspects, including British ones, under a form of house arrest or other restrictions in the community. Liberty has argued that these policies are profoundly unfair and therefore ultimately undermine security. They hand martyrs of injustice to the terrorist propagandists waiting to pounce on any apparent hypocrisy on the part of democrats. However, I have to concede that more immediately and narrowly, at least in the very short term, these devices can be said to pursue some attempted security goal (deportation, incarceration or restriction of movement).

Even this cannot be argued in defence of the closed proceedings of the Justice and Security Act, where all that is at stake is money, for example in the form of compensation for suspects who were rendered and tortured in freedom's name. This is about civil suits in civil courts. Trials in which, the government argues, it cannot adequately defend itself against allegations of wrongdoing without compromising national security and so would have to settle claims that it could fight and win on a secret one-sided playing field. What is strange about this argument is that government cannot give a single example of the courts behaving insensitively to security concerns or ordering the disclosure of evidence that would put lives at risk. If a relevant piece of evidence in a civil claim were too sensitive to disclose, the courts have a long track record of protecting it with 'public interest immunity'. Further, it remains for the claimant to prove their civil claim on the balance of probabilities and without access to this sensitive and immune material. If the government paid out on torture claims, it must have believed that such claims had sufficient substance to be proved in court on a balance of probabilities without claimants having access to national secrets. What's more, when this was done in response to claims from former Guantanamo detainees in 2010, no government application for public interest immunity had even been made, let alone refused.

The Justice and Security Act is a landmark piece of legislation for all the wrong reasons. In it centuries of British civil justice built on the principle of equality have been trashed for cash and the avoidance of embarrassment. As one extremely senior former spy once said to me, 'I am not prepared to be a cash point.' Notice the 'I' in that statement. It wasn't the gentleman's own money, after all. This is what we were dealing with. The arrogance that came with the indignation. The sad lack of humility or reflection on the part of ordinarily unaccountable people when briefly embarrassed over torture by our judges. So they duly instructed their so-called political 'masters' to change the law, instead of changing their own methods and practices in order to avoid similar embarrassment in the future.

Sadly, torture and cover-up were not limited to the rendition programme and the metaphysical aspect of the War on Terror. They formed a part of our country's literal wars too. In September 2011 a long-fought-for public inquiry led by Sir William Gage – which had consisted of 115 days of hearings and heard from some 348 witnesses – found that a 26-year-old Iraqi civilian called Baha Mousa had been detained, tortured and beaten to death by soldiers of the 1st Queen's Lancashire Regiment. He had suffered ninety-three separate injuries. Crucially, while the Ministry of Defence and its lawyers had long tried to limit blame for the scandal to a few 'bad apples' in the army, it was quite clear that the fault was a systemic one. The ministry itself had allowed back into use five cruel interrogation techniques which had been banned way back in 1972 by Conservative Prime Minister Edward Heath in the context of the Northern Ireland troubles. In his findings, Sir William described this as 'corporate failure' on the part of the MOD. The techniques in question included lengthy hooding with sandbags; subjecting the prisoner to prolonged periods in stress positions (such as being made to sit in an imaginary chair); long periods of sleep deprivation; ritualized abuse such as kick-boxing people around the room, and other forms of beating.

When the case was litigated, the House of Lords ruled that the Human Rights Act applied to places beyond our shores over which the UK government had control, a view that senior MOD legal advisers fought as hard as they did the setting up of the Gage inquiry itself. The decision in *Al-Skeini and Others v Secretary of State for Defence* was as important for the protection of military personnel serving abroad as it was to civilian prisoners, and is resisted and used as an anti-human rights gripe even to this day. Once more, accidental and perhaps unlikely human rights heroes distinguished themselves as much as those at the heart of the security establishment brought shame upon their professions and institutions. Lieutenant Colonel Nicholas Mercer, now a Church of England vicar and a self-identified 'Shire Tory', is an obvious case in point. The army's chief legal adviser in Iraq following the 2003 invasion repeatedly questioned the army's use of cruel interrogation techniques as contrary to Human Rights Law. As with many US military lawyers who did their best to stand for democratic decency, even in Guantanamo, Lt Col Mercer stood up to his own hierarchy and paid a high personal and professional price.

In the spring of 2003 and six months before Baha was beaten to death, Lt Col Mercer had advised that a judge be sent to Iraq to supervise the handling of prisoners.

'My job was to protect soldiers from legal proceedings and the degradation of human beings,' he told *Guardian* defence and security journalist Richard Norton-Taylor after the Gage findings in 2011. But Mercer's advice wasn't merely ignored. His army career was ruined. He says that he was told to keep his mouth shut and even threatened with a complaint to the Law Society by the chief MOD legal adviser, Martin Hemming, who shamelessly briefed against Mercer as a 'flake' and a fantasist, even in later meetings with me. It's a particularly nasty tactic to threaten inconvenient lawyers with professional discipline, like 'playing the man and not the ball'. It would seem that the lawyer as 'company man' is not a tradition unique to the CIA or USA. Campaigning solicitor Phil Shiner, who spent many years of his life representing Baha Mousa's grieving family and securing the Gage inquiry, was similarly subjected to a campaign of more than whispering contempt. Subsequent cuts to legal aid, including residence requirements, will make it very much harder to bring the powerful to account for any similar abuse and cover-up in the future.

Mercifully, Mercer – who subsequently won a Liberty Human Rights Award for his moral courage and professional integrity – was eventually vindicated by the courts and military personnel are now trained in human rights values.

Not before time. My campaigning litigation colleague Emma Norton (nicknamed Brockovich in the office, after the tenacious American campaigner against injustice of that name) currently works on behalf of the families of young dead British military personnel – both those from the infamous Deepcut Barracks and Anne-Marie Ellement, who committed suicide after a rape complaint against her own military police comrades was ignored. At every turn, Norton faces resistance from a Ministry of Defence establishment that spins and briefs the media that human rights have no place on their patch. But she isn't arguing for a right to air-conditioning or cigarette breaks. She is arguing against inhuman and degrading treatment and unlawful killing and for justice for those, most of them young, who put their lives in peril with noble ideals at the direction of and in the care of the state.

There is of course a reason why torture and slavery are the two absolute human rights wrongs. They are two aspects of the same extreme degree of degradation and inhumanity. In 2007, we celebrated the bicentenary of the Slave Trade Act, under which sea captains were subject to fines for every slave found on board their ships. The story of the campaign for this seminal piece of legislation is beautifully brought to life in the wonderful Michael Apted film *Amazing Grace*, starring, among others, Liberty stalwart Benedict Cumberbatch (many years before *Sherlock* and the phenomenal success that followed). However, despite the vital moral statement and ambition of that legislation, it was not actually a criminal offence to hold someone as a slave in Britain until Liberty successfully campaigned for section 71 of the Coroners and Justice Act in 2009.

Prior to this, if you locked someone up, it was 'false imprisonment'. If you beat or threatened them, there were various offences against the person. But often the bruises heal long before the victim emerges from the shock and finds the courage to make a criminal complaint. And what if you had other means of controlling the vulnerable on account of their immigration status or fears for loved ones far away or other forms of psychological vulnerability? Working with grass roots anti-slavery groups such as Kalayaan and Anti-Slavery International, my legal colleague Corinna Ferguson found a culture of complacency and neglect on the part of the police and prosecution authorities failing to take up the cases of the modern-day slaves held against their will in British homes.

They included her client Patience Asuquo. She came to London from Nigeria aged twenty-two in 2004 and worked as a domestic servant for a solicitor practising in the capital. Given what followed, her employer's profession is worth bearing in mind.

In the three years running up to the bicentenary of the Slave Trade Act, Patience's passport was held by her employer. She was subjected to regular verbal and physical abuse and paid no more than about £2,000 during the entire period of her employment, which worked out at less than £14 a week. She lived in fear until, in August 2007, she finally escaped and was able to make a complaint to the Metropolitan Police, only to be told, just over a year later, that the investigation was closed. But Article 4 of the Convention and Human Rights Act places the state under a positive duty to protect people from slavery. In response to legal proceedings – a judicial review – brought by my colleagues in 2009, the Metropolitan Police were forced to accept that they were in breach of the Human Rights Act and agreed to reopen the investigation.

This story proved vital to our campaign for the creation of a new criminal offence of holding another person in slavery or servitude or requiring them to perform forced or compulsory labour. This campaign was ably championed in the House of Lords by the fearless cross-bencher Baroness Lola Young. While the pre-election Brown government was eventually persuaded, we initially met significant resistance from officials in that administration. When you watch news reports of shocking Crown Court trials and convictions of people who held the vulnerable, often the learning disabled, as modern-day slaves; when you hear many of the current politicians who cast themselves as latter-day Wilberforces by banging on about the evils of slavery while simultaneously slating the Human Rights Act; remember what the media and politicians rarely tell you. Remember my colleague Corinna, her brave client Patience and that it was the Human Rights Act 'what won it'.

Torture and slavery have yet to be consigned to history, even in twenty-first-century Britain. Tragically, even lawyers have been complicit in grave abuses and have made too many of the excuses for them. Nonetheless, the absolute protections against them in the Human Rights Act have proved vital, both at home and abroad. And this often to the severe irritation and embarrassment of the powerful. Yet, I have not fully responded to the ticking nuclear bomb scenario – that question that follows me around like a shadow – have I?

So let's play the game and paint the picture of a gripping Benedict Cumberbatch blockbuster of the large or small screen. In fairytale number one I am the prime minister (I know, I know, you're really going to have to work with me on this one), who receives the telephone call from a foreign friendly power with a murky record on and approach to human rights. A horrific plot to kill millions somewhere in Britain has been uncovered and a suspect identified, quite possibly by the torture of her associates in another land. Do I pass the intelligence on to the commissioner of the metropolis so as to facilitate an urgent investigation and the suspect's possible arrest? Yes, I do. I know that material gleaned from torture will not stand up in a UK court, but the test for arrest is only reasonable suspicion and I must hope that our policing professionals will find intelligence and evidence to either incriminate or exculpate the suspect, or at least foil the anticipated plot.

That's the easy one! I hear you shout. What about the final act? Now I am the cop or the spook alone in the room with the gloating suspect straight from central casting, who taunts me with the ticking nuclear bomb but will not reveal its location in time to save a city. We can even give her a sadistic and cynical laugh if you like, or a hook for a hand and a patch over one eye. Do I find some clever way to persuade or trick the villain into revelation? Do I bribe or blackmail? What else do I do? Do I, fast running out of time, resort to violence against the suspect? How can I possibly know? What I do know is that the law against abusive interrogation and torture must be left unchanged, and that I should make whatever calm or desperate personal ethical decision in the knowledge of its full weight and consequences for everyone – including myself.

If I choose the path of cruelty over ingenuity and thereby save millions, I will no doubt throw myself on the mercy of a jury and seek a 'perverse acquittal' in the face of the law and evidence against me. Some may hail me as an unlikely and reluctant hero and no doubt say they told me so about torture. But for fantasy scenarios where dark practices are acceptable and routine not to become reality, I must be required to weigh the grave potential consequences for me alongside those for the suspect. Neither a prime minister nor a judge should be able to dial up or sanction torture and I should never be able to argue that I was just following orders. That excuse for a chain of command ends humanity and responsibility for all concerned. It didn't work as a defence at Nuremberg in the last century and it should never be allowed in London, Washington or anywhere else in this supposedly more enlightened age.

6

Rubbing Along Together

Oh, I love this city! I love it. Wherever I go in the world, to land back in London is the best feeling. I get to see so many amazing places when I'm working, like Miami, and I think, I could live here. But then I go, Yeah, but I wouldn't be in London.

— Amy Winehouse (interviewed by
Paul Du Noyer for *The Word* magazine)

My mother died on 23 July 2011, the same morning 27-year-old Amy Winehouse was found dead in her London home. Although she lived to the age of sixty-nine, my mum's life was a story of opportunity unfulfilled, in large part because of the discrimination that a woman of her generation had to endure. She was born and brought up in India and then lived all her adult life in the United Kingdom. She displayed a gift for singing and acting at an early age but her father refused to let her take up early exciting possibilities of pursuing her talents. She came to London and married my father in the early 1960s but, despite a natural charm, eloquence and university education, was held back in any career ambitions beyond retail, mostly because of the lack of affordable quality childcare. Then, in the final decade of her life, poor vision and a stroke left her increasingly withdrawn. It was incredibly painful to see my gregarious mother disappear into herself, despite my dad's most loving efforts, retreating from the books, arts and socializing that had been her special joys.

My mum was never one of life's grumblers. She took different people, countries and cultures as she found them. Born into a Hindu family, she was evacuated to a Himalayan hill station from Calcutta during the Second World War, where she was educated by mostly Scottish and Irish Catholic nuns. This upbringing helped instil in my mum a healthy respect for people of all faiths and of none. It also equipped her to thrive in the bedsit land of 1960s London. Her friends were of every race and religion and – unusually perhaps for a woman of her background and generation – even over twenty-five years ago, my gay college friends received the warmest of welcomes in her home. If it takes a certain underlying optimism and faith in humanity to believe in human rights, this I inherited from her.

This type of faith, and a great deal of moral courage besides, will also be permanently associated with that 2011 weekend. In Norway, a man launched two horrific attacks in quick succession. First, he detonated a home-made fertilizer car bomb in front of the prime minister's office in Oslo, killing eight people and injuring over 200 others. A couple of hours later came the stuff of nightmare: the same man, heavily armed and dressed as a police officer and carrying false ID, gained access to the island of Utoya, where the Youth Wing of the Norwegian Labour Party was gathered. He claimed that he had come to provide extra security following the Oslo bombing. He then embarked on a shooting spree that killed sixty-nine people and injured well over 100. Predictably perhaps, some initially assumed that these atrocities were the work of Islamist terrorists. In fact the killer was a 32-year-old white man, Anders Breivik, a right-wing extremist driven by a hatred of Islam and Muslim migration to Western Europe.

Prime Minister Jens Stoltenberg's speech the following morning was worthy of a great statesman reassuring a country facing enormous grief. Vowing that the attacks would not harm Norwegian democracy, he told his people and the world that the answer to the violence was 'more democracy, more openness, but not naivety'.

This idea of openness without naivety is one with which the drafters of the European Convention on Human Rights would have been very comfortable after the horrors of the Second World War. For this framework of fundamental rights was never merely a clever lawyer's toolkit but a set of values to help us define the limits of both freedom and security, and, crucially, of tolerance and integration. It isn't, of course, a formula that can produce the perfect right answer to every societal tension or problem, but it can, in my experience, assist in the navigation of many a minefield. It can really help us rub along together.

As the daughter of Commonwealth migrants to Britain I have had obvious personal as well as professional cause to think about this concept of 'identity' that is so often and bitterly fought over. In fact it is sometimes used as a euphemism for fears about liberal values and immigration in particular. It seems to me that we tend to see so-called identity in one of two ways.

The first is that of the military checkpoint or border control where we are required to present our passport, identity card or other papers that define us in the fixed ideological terms that the state or military have imposed. In these cases, we're identity checked by people in uniform who are often armed with weapons. We may be questioned. If our answers don't satisfy or we seem out of place, we might be taken aside for further interrogation. We may be searched, even intimately.

Facing all this, we may become nervous and that anxiety might appear to be suspicious. We may very well feel more than a little degraded and even angry. The whole experience is difficult, confrontational and possibly humiliating, but it determines whether or not we are allowed to pass and therefore on which side of the border we will be after this encounter. There is a single outcome: win or lose. Which side are you on?

The alternative – and here, not for the first time, I'm holding myself up to potential ridicule as a 'bourgeois liberal' – is the supermarket checkout. Think of one of those inner-city shops that's a cross between a supermarket and a convenience store where we go to pick up a few things after work. We fill our basket and if it's busy and there's a bit of a wait, people's eyes might wander on to what we're planning to buy. They may even make certain assumptions about who we are based on the contents of our last-minute shop. However, subject to our financial means that are of course a big consideration to take into account, the contents of our basket, at least, reflect decisions that we ourselves have taken.

One day I spot a young man in a sharp suit with a bottle of champagne. Do I recognize him instantly as a manual worker making a special effort for his mother's birthday or do I make assumptions about his life of privilege? My own basket might be just as likely to reflect my love of blue cheese as that of my mum's cooking. I sometimes buy microwavable curries because I miss her and don't have much time for cooking myself. The goods I buy vary according to circumstance and context.

Just like all of us, I am many things. I am a woman. I am a single parent, a friend, lawyer and campaigner. I am British, Asian and a Londoner. Which of these is most important to me at any particular moment may depend on whose company I am in or who I'm trying to connect with. My recent personal, political or social experiences will have an effect, as will a whole range of internal or external factors. In my view, this is the reality of human identity as opposed to the reductionist identity politics that force people to live under often arbitrary labels. The tough tactics of dead-end identity politics don't just split the countries and communities we might imagine they are designed to unite; they can leave an individual torn apart, with all the associated pain and resentment that will flow as a consequence. Victimhood is a terrible place and people do terrible things to one another in the name of 'identity'. It isn't just

Norman – now Lord – Tebbit's infamous cricket test of 1990 (in which, he proposed, the loyalty of British Asians to the United Kingdom would be impugned if they supported the subcontinent's national teams of their ancestry) or Mr Blair's ill-fated grandiose identity card folly that can have this effect. Nationalism and militarism divide loyalties. We may regard the colour of our passport, like that of our skin, as an important part of our identity, but that's our own individual choice. But why should a young man in Bradford identify with the suffering of fellow Muslims in Iraq or Palestine any less than I might with a mother struggling in sub-Saharan Africa? It's a foolish leader or policymaker who attempts to make citizenship or skin colour the whole or even predominant story in this ever more interconnected world of twenty-first-century human reality.

Religion and its obvious fault lines with other loyalties – our sense of our gender and sexuality in particular – are caught up in this divisive logic of identity politics. It seems that there are three ways of approaching the belief systems that are religions in our modern world.

The first option is to pick a religion, any religion. Make it your favourite, to the extent of embedding it into the fabric of your society, and legal and political systems. Everything else is secondary, even subordinate – in fact, ruthlessly so. The extreme modern example might be Afghanistan under the Taliban, but another illustration might be Britain, and not so very long ago.

Option number two is the opposite of the first, in which you treat all religious belief as dangerous and divisive mumbo-jumbo. In this view, religions are ultimately unenlightened and no good can ever spring from them. So we either ban religious belief altogether or, alternatively, chase it from the public into the private space. We allow it only in the church, mosque, temple or synagogue, or even just in the home – under the bed with the pornography. The extreme example here might be Stalin's Russia, a more moderate one today's French Republic.

You can guess, I am sure, from the way that I have

categorized, even caricatured, these two approaches, that I favour neither. And you'd be right. I think that a modern human rights attitude to religion in society looks – or should look – a little different. For me, the reality of human experience is that, however we choose to categorize ourselves, we are all creatures of both faith and reason, emotion and logic, albeit in variable proportions. Test it out. Even if we're deeply committed to our religion, we might still make calculations about all sorts of important matters affecting our family, finances, health and so on without any real reference to our holy script or spiritual guide. And even if we have no religious conviction and believe ourselves to be the most rational person in the world, we still make important decisions about who and what we like, even love, on the basis of instincts and emotions that have not been subject to calculation – even if we are clever enough to come up with a brilliant rational justification after the event, a process I have heard described as 'tock-tick logic'.

Throughout human history religious faith has helped to inspire prejudice and war and barely believable atrocities; inquisitions and crusades of various kinds. But religions have also inspired great works of art, from Mozart's *Requiem* to the Sistine Chapel, and much altruism and charitable giving. Equally, while logic, science and engineering produced the atom bombs and gas chambers of the last century, we have also used them to make unprecedented progress in the treatment of disease and to make people's lives longer and easier.

I believe that a human rights approach to religion confers on it neither privileged nor pariah status. It recognizes that freedom of thought, conscience and religion is a fundamental human right. As with privacy and even speech this freedom needs to be balanced with and qualified by the rights and freedoms of others, but it is no less important for that. In the United Kingdom religious tolerance has a long tradition as the right to the faith of your choice, the right to hold no faith and, perhaps most importantly, the right to be a heretic in any faith community. The right to religious freedom and expression should have protected Gurpreet Kaur Bhatti and her play *Behzti* (in Punjabi, *Dishonour*). The work caused offence to some Sikhs by depicting scenes of rape and violence in a Sikh temple. After violent protests outside the Birmingham Repertory Theatre on the opening night in December 2004, the play was cancelled. Religious freedom should protect the gay Christian and the Muslim seeking liberal and tolerant interpretations and applications of religious texts and customs. Today's heresy can become tomorrow's orthodoxy and I am reliably informed that the New Testament records Jesus' crime as that of blasphemy.

How does this all work to practical effect in our lives, families and communities? By reminding us that all of our fundamental rights and freedoms are interconnected. And also that we should be careful what we wish for. The cleric who seeks to ban satirical plays or cartoons should reflect on the counter-view: those who propose that what should really be banned are his own clothing or sermons. The aggressive secularist who seeks to outlaw the speech or garb of those he finds alien and unenlightened should reflect on what this says about his own beliefs.

My feminist heart does not exactly leap with joy when I see a woman covered from head to foot in an abaya and niqab. But neither am I ecstatic at pictures of young topless girls served up in the same tabloids that would have paedophiles hanged, drawn and quartered. I once shared this sentiment with a well-known tabloid newspaper that asked me to comment on its view that my position against burka bans made me a hypocritical or 'so-called' feminist. Perhaps unsurprisingly, the newspaper in question never printed my quote.

In both cases, I worry about how voluntary and consensual these women's choices really are. I have talked with confident and articulate young women who tell me that their religious observance or glamour modelling has been about following their own positive spiritual or economic path. In any event, it's essential to question the efficacy of banning these codes of religious dress that I fail either to fully understand or agree with. If there are bruises under a woman's burka, how does criminalizing her dress do anything other than trap her at home? And if it really is an exploitative boyfriend who urges her to bare all in the newspaper, isn't it better to have the argument and empower the woman rather than to drive the economic and sexual exploitation further and more dangerously underground?

I can live with what I find difficult and detest, even if only to have the opportunity to challenge it openly in lively debate. As Matt Santos, the fictional successor to President Bartlet in Aaron Sorkin's *The West Wing*, said when talking about the US Constitution and religion: 'This wasn't designed to make us comfortable. It was designed to keep us free.' Or, if you prefer, the words attributed to Jesus in Matthew's Gospel: 'Judge not, that ye be not judged. For with what judgment ye judge, ye shall be judged: and with what measure ye mete, it shall be measured to you again.'

I defend your right to foam at the mouth from the pulpit or soapbox and to irritate, offend and insult me, even to the point of preaching that I am a lesser creature than you. You should be able to bar me from your home, church or clergy, if that is your taste, view or faith. That is your freedom of speech, conscience, association and your private life. That is your loss not mine.

Obviously there have to be limits to this freedom and tolerance. Absolute liberty for the lion is tyranny for the lamb. There should be necessary and proportionate limitations to our freedoms, but only when those freedoms begin to impact on others. At this point, the limits should be tightly drawn.

By this measure, we get to choose who you can admit to our church, political party and home. But when our church offers adoption services to the wider public, or when we convert our home into a B&B, we do not get to discriminate against people of different faith, race, gender or sexuality. It can't be as simple as some kind of public–private divide. We do not get to be cruel to our children, even in the privacy of our own home; but by the same principle, neither should we be forced to take off our cross or turban just because we're walking down a public street. This is about whether we are really hurting, as opposed to offending, other people. It concerns the balance between our autonomy and freedom on the one hand, and another person's on the other.

I appreciate that these are difficult balances to strike. The correct approach to them, in my view, is that the person interfering with another's freedom is the one who has to justify their behaviour, according to the principles I've just outlined. This is an important rule. Generally speaking our clothing in public, or even at work, will not cause harm to others. However, there may well be exceptions related to security or our ability to do our job. I believe we should be able to wear a burka in the street and while sorting post at work, but we may need to be identified against our passport in an appropriate and discreet manner at the airport. Wearing a burka may not be ideal for vocations that depend on trust or non-verbal communication – teaching small children, say, or practising medicine. Equally the religious symbol on a chain around your neck should generally not be a problem, even at work. But if you are a surgeon, working in a sterile environment, it makes obvious sense that you should be required to take it off before you scrub down.

I defend the right of anyone to believe in and campaign for different social and legal orders which prohibit same-sex or interracial marriage(what's the difference?). However, someone who has chosen to be a civil registrar should not be able to pick and choose which ceremonies to conduct any more than the non-conscript soldier can choose which wars to fight. Overt discrimination in the offering of goods and services to the public, meanwhile, does real harm. Two queues, or front and back entrances on the basis of an unchangeable personal quality is degrading and dangerous. They did harm in the once-segregated

South of the United States. They did harm in apartheid South Africa and in the United Kingdom of the 1950s and 60s, when shopkeepers put signs saying 'No blacks, dogs or Irish' in their windows. They did harm when gay couples were turned away from hotels and B&Bs. The men who took those innkeepers to court, with the help of my colleagues at Liberty, were as important as Rosa Parks refusing to move to the back of the bus.

There will always be a degree of difficulty and controversy about where the proportionate limitations on our liberties should be drawn. The Human Rights Act is a compass not a computer – but it works for everyone. We rub along better by tolerating and, better still, respecting difference of all kinds. And in so doing we discover our similarities as much as our differences and the common humanity that binds us together.

The dehumanization of debate is rarely as evident as in rows about immigration and asylum. At times it is hard to believe that immigrants from the former British Empire, like my parents, were once actively invited to Britain, recruited to boost the economy and provide vital public services. Equally, refugees were often seen as noble or even heroic figures. They were defecting spies, athletes and ballet dancers from behind the Iron Curtain, whose risky journeys to freedom in the West made us feel better about our society and ourselves.

It's not my place, task or ambition to advise on the precise levels of immigration that Britain or any other economy should implement. But it's important to emphasize – because they're often treated as being somehow less than fully human – that migrant workers are human beings too. They are not disposable tools to be bought, sold and segregated from the rest of the population. This is what happens to the euphemistically termed 'guest workers', who have been treated as a lower form of life throughout history and all over the world. But, as we all do, migrant workers inevitably form personal and cultural relationships in the places to which they travel and where they live and work. They find, lose and re-find work (most often work that the citizens of the host country are unwilling to do themselves). They settle and raise families, as my parents did. Children like me have never known a home other than the one established by their parents in the country to which they travelled, sometimes at great personal cost.

There are certain levers of immigration control which are damaging, divisive, counterproductive and even unacceptable from a human rights perspective that must afford all humans a modicum of respect. It is wrong to leave people in a state of legal flux or limbo for long periods of time, thus stimulating underground economies that make the most vulnerable hostage to exploitation and slavery. It is wrong to split up families by expelling the parents of children born or long settled in their host country – or at least to do so without compelling reasons of public interest. It is wrong to deny people a fair hearing, including adequate legal advice, representation, translation and appeals, before parcelling them off across the world and changing their lives for ever. It is wrong – as public and even tabloid media opinion agreed in the context of the luminous Joanna Lumley's triumphant legal and political campaign for the Gurkhas in 2008–9 – to expect people to serve your country, at great personal risk and cost over many years, and then seek to exclude them when they seem less useful. If this is true of soldiers who fought under the British flag, it is as true of the unarmed interpreters who aided them or indeed of the many hard-working skilled professionals who have long staffed the NHS.

To move immigration control from the national border to the homes, schools, doctors' surgeries, restaurants and streets of Britain's cities, towns and villages seems to me a race relations time bomb. This kind of everyday monitoring was always my biggest concern about the proposed identity card system. And now, the very coalition government that did away with that dangerous and divisive measure is sanctioning a stepping up of in-country raids on buses and curry houses in our inner cities. In an ominous echo of the worst far-right propaganda of my childhood in the 1970s, it hired mobile billboards to drive around neighbourhoods with particularly rich ethnic mixes, warning 'over-stayers' to 'Go home or face arrest'. And it passed the Immigration Act 2014 that will force landlords and even vicars to check nationality or status before providing those who seek their services with housing or joining them in marriage.

Suppose, in a few years' time, my British son and the child of one of my white Liberty colleagues go looking to rent the same room, perhaps as students. How many landlords aren't going to err on the side of caution and give my colleague's kid the room? And, ironically, with the new immigration law, the government is proposing to do what it cautiously and rightly avoided, even when instituting same-sex marriage: it is interfering in the Church of England's prerogative to conduct marriage services. It is as if the 1970s and 80s never happened, as if we never fought for the Race Relations and Equality Acts. As with stop-and-search and other sources of discrimination, the Immigration Act will do enormous harm to the equality and solidarity that binds people, communities and countries together.

If the denigration of the 'ordinary immigrant' has been bad enough, that of asylum seekers and refugees has been far worse. If the entire modern universal human rights settlement owes its creation and content principally to the worst horrors of the twentieth century, this is surely especially true of the 1951 Refugee Convention. My great friend the respected human rights' academic and thinker Francesca Klug once described the Refugee Convention to me as 'the world's apology for the Holocaust'. This highly appropriate and necessary apology lasted for a while. In 1985 President Reagan, on visiting Bergen-Belsen concentration camp, made the following remark:

Freedom-loving people around the world must say ... I am a refugee in a crowded boat foundering off the coast of Vietnam. I am a Laotian, a Cambodian, a Cuban, and a Miskito Indian in Nicaragua.

Since then, haven't we moved a long way from this statement of empathy and identification with the refugee – let alone the international instrument crafted for her protection? Certainly, my adult life in Britain has been one of real progress, often fuelled by human rights litigation, on issues of race and gay equality in particular. On the global stage we have witnessed the historic end of apartheid in South Africa and the pulling down of the Iron Curtain across Europe. Yet simultaneously, respect for and protection of the world's refugees – including those created by modern militarism – have become more fragile than ever. In this, Britain appears to be an especially bad case in point.

This decline seems to have begun, at least according to Home Office folklore, in 1986, just a year after Reagan's celebrated speech at Belsen-Bergen, when fifty-four Sri Lankans got off a plane and claimed asylum at Heathrow airport. Was it that we didn't mind the principle of protecting refugees in the first safe country to which they escaped, as long as that country was across a land border somewhere far away in the so-called developing world? Was it that when air travel shrank the world for our convenience, we found it less than convenient that distances also shrank for asylum seekers and refugees? It can surely make as much or more sense for a persecuted individual to escape on a plane to a European country with colonial, cultural and linguistic ties to her own, or where there is already a happy and thriving community of people from her homeland, than to crawl over a land border to a country barely safer than her own. In terms of global justice, is it really so wrong that one of the richest countries in the world should take more than a fraction of the world's refugees, especially given that their past histories and present lives are directly or indirectly connected to its own imperial, or more recent, military adventures?

Instead, in recent decades, our politicians and sections of our press have undermined the 'worldwise' apology for the Holocaust, by quite literally dehumanizing refugees in thought, word and deed. In November 2001 the *Daily Express* wrote: 'Refugees are flooding into the United Kingdom like ants.' This was reminiscent of some of the worst propaganda leading up to the Rwandan genocide just seven years earlier, where Tutsis were described as cockroaches by the country's media outlet Radio Télévision Libre des Mille Collines.

Three years later in April 2004, Tony Blair addressed the Confederation of British Industry on migration and said that he thought the Convention had 'started to show its age' – as though it were a clapped-out car. He told them it was designed for a time when 'the cold war and lack of cheap air travel made long-range migration far more difficult than it has become today'. On Prime Minister Blair's watch it became, for the first time, a stated aim of government policy to reduce asylum applications, however compelling or worthy. The reason, he explained, was because the asylum process was being 'widely abused' and that was undermining our system and making it more difficult for those genuinely seeking asylum. The government put in place greater pre-embarkation controls at ports around the world, including in countries from where a number of obviously genuine refugees were coming. Much of this pre-border policing was farmed out and forced upon the airline companies. This preceded the more overt contracting-out of immigration control and removal to private companies that in years to come would insulate ministers from public outrage even when people died at the hands of brutal and ill-trained security guards.

In my early post 9/11 days as in-house counsel at Liberty, another dear friend and lifelong race equality champion, Lord

Lester of Herne Hill QC, phoned to gift me with my first case against my former employer, the Home Secretary. Anthony Lester had worked tirelessly for equality and other fundamental rights since the 1960s when, as Labour Home Secretary Roy Jenkins's special adviser, he had fought considerable institutional opposition to pave the way for the first Race Relations Act. He continues to campaign in the courts and in the House of Lords to this day. But the case we built together in 2001 with Dinah Rose, now a celebrated QC in her own right, was to be vital in its content and timing for the protection of his legacy.

By the summer of 2001 the Czech Republic had left its Communist past behind and was knocking on the door of the European Union, which it was to join three years later. But institutions such as the EU and the World Bank, when deciding on a country's stage of 'development', rarely look at its human rights record as closely as its economy.

Roma people were treated appallingly in the Czech Republic. They suffered the lowest levels of education, employment and housing in the country and were subject to routine discrimination. They were attacked by racist skinheads – as my parents once were with me in the pram in 1970 – and left unprotected by the state. Unsurprisingly, therefore, the newly developed Czech Republic was still producing large numbers of asylum seekers to the United Kingdom and elsewhere. A handful of these had managed to persuade even our sceptical and obstructive authorities that their treatment had been sufficiently bad to create a 'well-founded fear of persecution' if they were returned home.

On the other hand, the Czech Republic was 'open for business', and the British government was quite keen to welcome the newly affluent – and mostly white – Czech corporate and commercial class to come and do business in Britain. This type of situation inevitably creates tensions between the iron fist of our Home Department, with its instinct for locking down borders, and whatever the latest incarnation of the Department of Trade (currently the Department for Business, Innovation and Skills) might be.

Traditionally, departments will fight it out between themselves before government decides whether nationals of the country in question should have to apply for a visa. If border control interests win, visas will be required; if business triumphs, people will be able to come for a short visit without applying for a visa in advance. Once you are in the country, even if you originally said you were only visiting as a tourist, you can then claim refugee protection on the grounds of likely persecution back home. And if you do so, you – rightly – cannot be removed until your claim for asylum is properly considered.

But on this occasion in 2001, an ever-ingenious bureaucracy – at least, ever-ingenious when it comes to attempting to circumvent human rights legislation – tried to have its cake and eat it too. Visa requirements would not be placed on this soon-to-be EU-allied country – thus placating the business lobby. But pre-embarkation checks would be installed at Prague airport to weed out potential asylum seekers – so pleasing the Dark Tower. This was a deliberate and cynical attempt to get round one of the greatest protections of the post-Holocaust settlement; namely, that you let people escape – even in disguise, or on forged papers, or otherwise illegally – and decide the strength of a claim for protection in the country of safety. Under a deal with the Czech government, the UK border and its immigration officers were relocated to Prague to conduct racial profiling at the city's international airport for the purpose of keeping asylum seekers out of Britain.

Coming from a British Asian family, I was well aware that this was far from being the first time that the British authorities had degraded and dehumanized people in the name of immigration control. In the 1970s, before asylum seekers were considered a problem, the concern was to keep the arriving spouses of Commonwealth nationals out of the country. Hindu brides were therefore subjected to virginity testing at Heathrow airport. What informed these unbelievably intrusive checks was a cold, ruthless and racially discriminatory logic that ran as follows: the cultural norm in conservative Hindu communities was generally to abstain from sex before marriage. Therefore a woman who had already lost her virginity was less likely to be a 'genuine' bride. In fact, her 'primary purpose' in getting married was probably to gain entry to the UK. The scandal of these tests was revealed in a front-page exposé in the *Guardian*: its author was the then 28-year-old cub reporter Melanie Phillips.

Yes, that really happened. Young women were degraded in that way at Heathrow airport by British officials as recently as the 1970s. That's what results without a Human Rights Act to protect all humans, including foreign nationals, from inhumanity and degradation.

So when Anthony Lester brought the 2001 Prague airport 'experiment' to my attention I was – in the words of the *West Wing*'s President Bartlet himself this time – 'shocked but not surprised'. In fact, this sentiment is such a fitting response for so many outrages of recent years that Liberty's policy director, Isabella Sankey, and her young and inspiring colleagues have taken to signing off 'SBNS' at the bottom of emails about the latest government contempt for rights and freedoms.

Fortunately, though over three years later, a House of Lords Appellate Committee, again chaired by the late great Lord Bingham, came to our aid with the clear finding that the scheme breached the Race Relations (Amendment) Act 2000. It was just as well that they ruled that way in December 2004, for the London bombings of the following July brought vociferous calls for the institution of racial profiling. The chief of the Transport Police presumably thought he was being reassuring when he said that he didn't need to stop 'little white old ladies'. Various commentators called for overt racial profiling at airports, presumably unaware of the many white converts to the Jihadi cause, or the way that people of all physical descriptions can be turned into 'mules', 'human shields' and no doubt bombs when under sufficient duress.

Here, it's worth reflecting on the all-important 2000 Act, passed in the aftermath of Stephen Lawrence's murder and the policing scandal and McPherson Inquiry which followed. The Act took the principle of non-discrimination in the provision of 'goods and services' (in the private sector sense) into the heart of the state that is policing, prisons, border controls and related regulatory bodies. In the words of Baroness Hale of Richmond: 'The inevitable conclusion is that the operation was inherently and systematically discriminatory and unlawful.'

Lady Hale is another acute legal mind of the late twentieth and early twenty-first centuries. Like Tom Bingham, she possesses considerable human understanding; an essential, though seemingly less than universal quality for a judge in our country's highest court. Appointed the UK's first woman Law Lord in 2004, Lady Hale remains our first and only woman Justice of the Supreme Court since its institution in 2009. It could surely only help the practical and demographic legitimacy of the great guardian of the rule of law that is our senior judiciary, if the female population (over half the total population) could identify with it a little more easily? There should be more women. The current position is almost as embarrassing as the various excuses that are made for it. Justice must be seen to be done.

On a happier note, I will never detract from New Labour's achievements in developing the Northern Ireland peace process, from its important beginnings under the now Sir John Major. I also credit Mr Blair with great progress on gay equality legislation – though much of it merely caught up with attitudinal change already hard fought for and won. The most intimate and social of revolutions began in our homes and on

the streets in response to the Thatcherite homophobia encapsu-
lated in section 28 of the Local Government Act 1988. This
described same-sex partnerships as 'pretended family relationships', effectively censoring teachers and banning certain books
from our schools. The campaign that followed – so skilfully
driven by Angela Mason and her Stonewall team – also built on
a long tradition of successful cases brought under the
much-maligned right to respect for private life in the Court of
Human Rights.

It is no doubt some considerable achievement that Blair's
prime-ministerial-heir-but-one, the Conservative David Cameron, should feel confident enough in the culture shift of
modern Britain not just to leave civil partnerships alone, but to
institute same-sex marriage.

And even if Mr Blair never really loved, nurtured, promoted
or protected this particular child, he did see the Human Rights
Act passed in his first energetic term of office. Prime ministers
give and they take away. His attitude to the most desperate of
travellers that is the refugee does him absolutely no credit at all
and is perhaps even a little ironic in the light of his own subsequent life, travelling with ease through first-class airport
lounges and on private jets. Why should internationalism be
the preserve of the super-rich? Why just for multinational companies, the avoidance of tax and the movement of assets? Why
just for markets and money, but not for ordinary human beings,
including the most vulnerable who need their common values
and legal protections?

The world's refugees were sent a clear signal that they were
unwelcome in Britain. Now, new arrivals were subject to new
policies of forced destitution severely restricting financial and
other support. These measures were instituted in a snowy British winter. New too, was administrative detention, including of
rape and torture victims and their children. Centres originally
designed for humane reception, where newly arrived asylum

seekers could receive food, shelter, education, advice and have their claims quickly and fairly considered, were instead turned into vast detention centres. Refugees were imprisoned on arrival, purely for coming from a country on a Home Office 'white list'. This was the enacting of a policy of blanket detention of people whose claims had not even been initially decided. The government justified it on the basis that some of these people would eventually be found to be lying. In other words, all asylum seekers were to be assumed guilty until proved innocent. Isn't this rather like detaining the business community en masse pending the consideration of their corporate accounts and tax returns, on the basis that some of them will eventually be found to be cheats?

The Refugee Convention of 1951 always recognized that persecuted people may need to carry false papers and identities in order to flee persecution. However, from 2005 onwards there was greater general criminalization of asylum seekers and more prosecutions. Fingerprinting. Electronic tagging. And imprisonment. Their access to healthcare was severely cut back, as was access to legal advice and appeals. This, even though so many of them had revealed the very poor standard of initial decision-making in cases where people's lives were quite literally at risk if wrongly returned. To cap it all, such treatment was meted out to refugees escaping conflicts in which Britain was still participating, namely Afghanistan and Iraq.

Helena Kennedy (Baroness Kennedy of The Shaws) QC has been one of my role models for pretty much as long as I can remember. A criminal barrister with humble roots in Glasgow, she is one of the few great lawyers with a gift for plain English that has been as brilliantly deployed in decades of broadcasting as in jury trials. With her skills and lifelong support of the Labour Party, it was no surprise that she should be ennobled in 1997, an obvious candidate for a working peerage. But her equally strong human rights and rule of law values brought her into direct collision with New Labour's anti-civil liberties agenda. When conscience prevailed over tribal loyalty a few times too many, the 'Red Baroness' found herself painfully ostracized from old and dear Labour friends, including many in the House of Lords. But she stuck to her guns and does so still. Not long ago, she reminded me that as recently as 2001, the then Home Secretary Jack Straw was refusing asylum to opponents of Saddam Hussein.

In her book *Just Law*, Kennedy cites a 2002 *New Statesman* report of a Home Office refusal letter to an asylum seeker, which still makes for chilling reading:

> The Secretary of State has at his disposal a wide range of information on Iraq which he has used to consider your claims. He is aware that Iraq, and in particular Iraqi security forces, would only convict and sentence a person in the courts with the provision of proper jurisdiction. He is satisfied, however, that if there are charges outstanding against you and if they were to be proceeded with on your return, you could expect to receive a fair trial under an independent and properly constituted judiciary.

Helena's comment is pithy: 'Tell that to the families of those exhumed from mass graves.'

As I write, the coalition government is prevaricating over accepting anything but a small number of refugees from the bloody civil war in Syria, a conflict in which Mr Cameron was eager to intervene on humanitarian grounds. Why should human rights violations so often be used as justification for war 'over there', but not for protection over here – in our home?

I believe this over-there/over-here emotional disjunction is out of sync with the instinctive response of people everywhere, not least in Britain. Look at the way that public charitable responses to natural disasters around the world put our governments to shame. Look at the way that small local and community anti-deportation campaigns run counter to populist political rhetoric and depressing opinion polls. When strangers move into our street and their kids play with our own, they are soon strangers no more. But if they remain seg-regated and stigmatized – barred from living and even working with us despite the skills and expertise that most bring from their pre-conflict lives – they can become dehumanized aliens vulnerable to the politics of fear.

Ronald Reagan only called himself a refugee to make a point. But Olympic gold-medal runner and national hero Mo Farah really was a refugee. So is my friend Camila Batman-ghelidjh. A child of enormous wealth and privilege in pre-revolutionary Iran, she became a refugee while at board-ing school in England and went on to found and run Kids Company – an awe-inspiring charity which looks after some of the most deliberately forgotten children in our country. All these years, she has retained her refugee status rather than become a citizen, in solidarity with those less fortunate. The Milibands' father, the left-wing intellectual Ralph Miliband, fled the Nazis. This list goes on and on. The tales of the extra-ordinary contributions to society made by refugees and their children continues throughout history and the world. These are real people, not scary statistics. Many braved grave dangers and endured enormous hardship to leave their homeland and start a new life in often bewilderingly different circumstances.

Back in 1996, when I was a young Home Office immigration lawyer, Pardeep Saini, a 22-year-old from India, survived a ten-hour flight clinging to the undercarriage of a plane; his younger brother Vijay died of hypothermia. Should we not reflect on the kind of experiences that prompt such desperation, in the same way that, on 9/11, those trapped in the nightmare of the Twin Towers preferred to jump from them rather than wait for the alternative? I remember my father – who had by then been naturalized from Indian to British citizenship for many years – phoning me up about these two young men. He no doubt recalled that he himself had been in his early twenties when he came, quite lawfully, to London at the invitation of the Macmillan government. 'I shall be ashamed if they don't let that young man stay,' he told me. 'He deserves my British passport, more than I do.' Having the privilege of being born in Britain, I did even less to acquire my passport than my dad did. I know what he meant. Do you?

In the summer of 2012, the Olympics finally came to London. I had the awesome privilege, on Liberty's behalf, of carrying one corner of the Olympic flag into the stadium. I walked alongside Doreen Lawrence and Sally Becker – 'the Angel of Mostar', who risked her life to save hundreds of others during the conflicts in Bosnia and Kosovo – among other heroic figures from around the world. Looking around, I was acutely aware that they were infinitely more worthy of the honour than me. The ceremony that preceded this moment was a beautiful reminder of how strongly our vibrant multiculture had featured in London's bid to host the Games. It was even more poignant when one remembers the attack on our great open and diverse city that came the day after the bid was won.

Danny Boyle's extravaganza was a sight to behold. There was no hint of the pomp and military-style uniformity of the Beijing Games that – some had feared – the 'Big Smoke' would be unable to follow. And yet, what a display of a different kind of power in the modern world. Shakespeare was celebrated, but so were the suffragettes. The Industrial Revolution was remembered in a particularly theatrically ingenious spectacle, but so was the *Windrush*. There was Elgar and punk, while the NHS and the internet were rightly highlighted as great free treasures of British design. This was the soft power of diversity and ingenuity and values, confidently displayed to the world. This ceremony set the tone for a wonderful summer of internationalism and sport, culminating in perhaps an even more inspiring and prejudice-busting Paralympic Games. This was our country rubbing along together, a country that aspired to be the equal of any, but no one's superior – except perhaps on the field of sporting battle.

Amy Winehouse didn't live to sing at the Olympics in her

beloved London (it's hardly fanciful to suggest that she would have been asked). However, the equally beautiful and talented young Emeli Sandé sang like an angel, aged just twenty-five. My mother never lived to see those Olympics in the adopted city where she lived for most of her life. But I wore some Indian pearls she had given me to the opening ceremony that summer. And, somehow, I think, she might have been proud.

Conclusion: The Case for Human Rights

They are largely a shoal species and therefore can out-compete the more individual trout.
— Wikipedia's description of *thymallus thymallus*
(the fish otherwise known as 'grayling')

Don't it always seem to go
That you don't know what you've got
Till it's gone
— 'Big Yellow Taxi' by Joni Mitchell

Some say we human beings have come to dominate the Earth because we were chosen by God. Others would say it's down to a particularly primeval, competitive and ruthless streak which allows us to impose our will on others and to drag the more vulnerable among us to the outskirts of the encampment to wither. I have no doubt about the beauty, creativity and ingenuity that come with our rugged individuality. But how could we have achieved so much, over thousands of years and against such difficult odds, without learning to bring our individual strengths together? How could we have built communities and even empires on a global scale, without imagining both the pain and potential of total strangers? Without solidarity as well as self?

I have a friend from my teenage years who is one of the

all-round best people I know. While it is sadly not always the case, isn't it lovely when the person you knew and loved in their youth grows up to be the person they were somehow always meant to be; someone that both you and their younger self would recognize, and of which both can be proud? I am lucky enough to have a number of friends like this, and I believe that is the potential for each of us. That is the promise of each new-born baby and newly arrived asylum seeker, and everyone else besides. Not because someone else, some member of a powerful elite, has judged us worthy. Just because we are human and alive. This is the potential that human rights values protect.

Human rights laws can protect us from premature death and wholly avoidable degradation, from modern-day slavery and unlawful detention. They guarantee fairness in the courtroom, where no one wants or expects to be but any one of us could find ourselves one day. Human rights laws safeguard privacy, intimacy and family life. They protect a free conscience and the creativity that can flow from it. They defend free association and expression and the vital democratic action and participation in a good society that are otherwise impossible. Any modern bill of human rights worth the ink must protect other people's children from all corners of the planet. Otherwise, how can our own children really be protected? Dignity, equality and fairness, and the greatest of all qualities which is empathy.

Some years ago my old friend's parents asked me to give one of a series of guest talks at their synagogue. I had admired them and their daughter all my adult life and accepted the invitation in a heartbeat. My friend's mother had survived a Nazi death camp and her father a Siberian work camp. Both eventually came to Britain, where they made enormous contributions to research, teaching and civil society, not least via the legacy of their three children, by now all middle-aged like me. As usual there was tight security at the entrance to the hall in which

I made my opening remarks. I always enjoy the debate more than the lecture, and was comfortable with some pretty robust comments from the audience about how to deal with terrorism in the Q and A that followed. The rather polite rough and tumble was nothing compared to questioning on mainstream radio and TV current affairs programmes. 'Why should we respect the rights of people who hate us?' 'Surely those who attack other people should lose their own protection.' That sort of thing. But I could see my friend's dear old dad gradually becoming indignant on my behalf. When he could contain himself no more, he rose to his feet in a moment that I will never forget. 'My wife was in a death camp and I was in Siberia,' he said. 'No one is going to tell me we don't need human rights laws.'

So here I sit in the second decade of the twenty-first century. I live in a country and a world of common values, humanity and great and righteous freedom struggles, many of them making real progress. But I also sense an atmosphere where, quite bizarrely, terror or complacency or both might tempt us to relinquish some of our most precious treasures. It is remarkable how often fear and ignorance come together. We can be so obsessed with threats to our lives from outside our community or society that we forget how easily we undermine them from within.

Unthinkingly, and at the instigation of those with obvious vested interests in keeping their power unchecked, we might lose hard-won fundamental rights that earlier generations paid for in courage and blood. I do not trust the powerful. Not because they are inevitably malevolent or venal, but because they are human, with all the frailty, fear and vanity that comes with humanity and all its many virtues. Do you write blank cheques often? Can you afford to?

We've watched, it seems, the near death of privacy. This has come from two directions, in a powerful pincer movement to which we are only just waking up. First, there is the predictable and insatiable appetite of those in power, in business or government. It is a hunger for more and more intimate information about the details and patterns of our lives. I understand why those who snoop for a living must get used to life in the shadows and working by stealth. Sadly, this has extended to massive spy programmes directed at entire populations on both sides of the Atlantic and beyond. This would seem to have been sanctioned and operated with contempt for and no recourse to the democratic niceties of public knowledge, political discussion and debate – let alone legal authority. We are told just to trust them, told 'Nothing to hide, nothing to fear'. But we all have something to protect, if not hide. Information is power and, as we have seen, unchecked power will inevitably be abused by accident or design.

Secondly, there is the rise of what some of my younger friends and colleagues think of as 'cool technology', whether it's social media or the apps dependent on knowing our location. They bring fun and convenience, but are also capable of real abuse. The toy that tells us where our nearest pizza can be bought will also tell others where we are. Of course it's ultimately incumbent on us not to let the state become our 'Big Brother'. But corporations and even individuals inspired by profit, or just prurience, are capable of being less than sweet siblings as well. Brand-new parents come home from hospital to find unordered complimentary samples of infant formula on their doorstep. Insecure or jealous spouses hack their loved ones' email accounts for tell-tale signs.

We've seen how bad and sloppy laws drafted for one – at least publicly stated – purpose can be used in unlikely or ingenious ways that were never imagined at the time they were passed, often during an apparent crisis and often almost on the cross-party nod. Naïve adventurers on the internet and other unlikely characters have been parcelled off around the globe and peace protesters dealt with like terrorists.

Fair trials, whether in the criminal or civil courts, have been treated like once beautiful but now battered antiques, worthy of little more than scrap. And this by many of the people who will no doubt queue up to wrap themselves in the Magna Carta as its 800th anniversary approaches. If the late Baroness Thatcher was once accused by a predecessor of 'selling the family silver', think of how some of her successors have trashed even the constitutional foundations of our home. Surely the right to a fair trial is no less glorious when, in the post-war era, it is translated from its original Latin into English and, via the European Convention, into many other languages besides? More importantly, even if available in modern English rather than an ancient tongue, the law becomes a dead letter in a sealed book in a land where only the rich and the powerful can afford access to fearless and independent legal advice and representation.

We have seen all kinds of 'otherness' defined and then predictably denigrated. 'Divide and rule' was once an imperial tool but it works still, and all too well, for the powerful all over the world to this day. You don't have to have been literally born to rule, it would seem, to act that way. It is too easy to acquire the knack of distracting those you serve from your practical difficulties and possible inadequacies, by turning them on each other at community, national or global level. No unity for us, no scrutiny for them. It's quite a combination. Other people's children should have ASBOs. Ours should have extra Maths tutoring instead. Our citizens should be protected by our laws, but when other governments want to persecute us under their laws – after all we are not their citizens – our friendly government will happily make the trade. Whether this comes at the price of our privacy or even protection from torture, it just gets waved through.

As if only to help further with my case for human rights rather than citizen's privileges, the same night that I write this the coalition government has added powers to its latest Immigration Act to strip British national 'suspects' of their citizenship, even if this would render them stateless. What did I warn of at the start of my story? Whether it's blanket surveillance, or internment and even torture, first it starts with the foreign nationals – and we are all foreigners in someone else's eyes. Now it seems our government wants to remind us that citizenship is a privilege bestowed by the political community. What politics gives, it can take away. Our common humanity is all we have left and we should protect it with our imagination and empathy, with our values and ultimately with law at home and internationally.

That's the ultimate essence of the Human Rights Act. It does what it says on the tin. But what do its enemies claim the problems to be?

First they say that the European Convention from which it derives is just somehow too, well, European. Like Berlusconi or Bratwurst or driving on the wrong side of the road. But the Convention itself was Winston Churchill's post-war legacy and Conservative lawyers played a major part in its drafting, thinking they were sharing thoroughly British values with younger and frailer democracies in post-war Europe.

Then they say that either the European Convention or the Human Rights Act, or both, have given away our national sovereignty. They are deliberately vague about which they have the bigger problem with. So let's take each instrument in turn. Yes, the European Convention is a treaty that binds our government under international law. But what is the problem with international law protecting everyone from torture, arbitrary detention, snooping, censorship and discrimination? If these values are good enough to form the charge sheet against governments elsewhere 'over there', why not our own dear government that we want held to account for our own protection? Haven't we seen how even continental judges of mixed quality in a Strasbourg Court are capable of protecting rights and freedoms – privacy in particular – that we were in danger of letting go by default? The Court of Human Rights gives a great deal of latitude to domestic politicians and judges to implement these values according to our own norms and traditions. Understandably, however, a brash reverse and altogether non-Churchillian two-finger salute just won't do, even when we don't like or understand every decision. It can't work in any club of like-minded people.

How can we and our judges help shape international law by pulling out of it? There is value in states, like people, putting up with irritation for the bigger picture and longer view. By staying in the Convention, we get to help guide its development with our own thinking. And, in turn, that is how we can influence the human rights thinking of the wider world. To put it another way, what kind of signal would a once mighty empire send to the rest of the world by pulling out of its most enforceable document of international human rights standards?

The Human Rights Act is the law that gives our judiciary the power to referee on Convention rights here at home. It means people in Britain need not wait up to a decade for access to a busy European Court that has been the victim of its own success in challenging so much state abuse. So the Act does the very opposite of ceding power to Europe.

Alternatively, they say that our human rights laws give away parliamentary sovereignty to unelected judges. But haven't we seen case after case of independent judges doing vital work in holding our politicians to account? As already illustrated, Parliament is too often dominated by government. In any event, if a Parliament is clear and committed enough, even in a desire to trample our rights and freedoms, declarations from the courts under the HRA have only a shaming and not an enforceable effect. Pretty tame stuff, you might think. If our political masters – supposedly our servants – find this too rich and testing for their blood, what kind of bill of rights could they possibly find acceptable and what could it possibly do to protect us?

Finally, they promise new mythical and magical bills of rights that would protect only the worthy and never the wicked. Haven't we seen these distinctions in the eyes of various beholders? Wicked prisoners shouldn't have the vote. Really? Not any one of them, no matter how short the sentence or questionable the crime? What if you chose to go to prison rather than take the identity card forced on you by a future authoritarian government? You paid the price for your protest with your liberty and some would say that's a democratic contract. But how democratic is it that you shouldn't even be able to vote from your cell for a party that opposes identity cards? And even if your crime were more conventional and your incarceration justified by your alleged dangerousness, how does depriving you of the vote provide public protection, your rehabilitation or punishment, or act as a real deterrent to others?

When so many people are tired of politics and fail to bother to vote, it hardly seems like true punishment or deterrence. Sadly, perhaps, can you really imagine a putative opportunistic thief put off from stealing either a loaf of bread or priceless diamonds for fear of missing out on the next general election? If prison is to be anything other than a dustbin or 'too-difficult pile' for forgotten humanity, how can the signal that people inside just do not count help in any nobler aim? Even if you don't agree with me and think that 'law breakers cannot be law makers', except when our leaders are breaching our rights and international law, is this the issue over which you would throw the baby out with the bath water and give up your own rights with those of the prisoners?

The bottom line is whether you choose a partisan politician or an independent judge to decide the limits of our basic human protections. Do you rely on goodwill and popular politics alone when it is you or your loved ones, quite literally, on the line?

Dear Reader, whether you have read my whole case or just skimmed it, whether you started or finished supportive, sceptical or downright seething, you have kindly indulged me for long enough. You have listened for some hours of your own precious life, which, let's face it, you are never getting back. I have told you about lots of different people, young and old, passed and still living, heroes and occasional villains, much admired colleagues and friends. Forgive me remembering one more dear one, who so encouraged me to write this book.

Dame Juliet Wheldon CB QC was the chief government lawyer and, before that, my boss, when I was young and worked in the Dark Tower. She was a consummate public servant of independence and discretion, including when we became close friends in the final years of her all too short life. I never knew if or how she voted and she never asked me if or where I put my cross. Juliet was a brilliant woman of talent and privilege, her greatest privilege probably being her amazing first-rate brain. This clever lawyer could have used her gifts to make financial fortunes for herself and others. But instead she chose public service and the Human Rights Act passed under Home Office sponsorship and on her watch. In her manner she was so English, at times reminding me of great cultural icons such as Joyce Grenfell or Penelope Keith, but she also loved to travel, initially to Italy in particular, but later further afield, to India and even some less than safe spaces in the Middle East.

A career public servant, she faithfully advised governments of both persuasions, without fear or favour but with enormous respect for the democratic authority of those who put themselves up for and win the public vote. She watched my transition to Liberty with interest and sometimes amusement and she didn't agree with me on every difficult issue, but she did agree on the value of protecting the European Convention and Human Rights Act at all costs. We two friends originated on different continents and had no blood relationship. You will no doubt have friends like this too. We were united by common humanity, humour and experience, and much more besides. I will not say that it was the law that united us, but an ultimate respect for it didn't hurt. As I hope I have demonstrated, when it comes to protecting human beings, and the underlying values that most of us ultimately hold dear, a little hard-edged legal protection can make all the difference in the world.

In Liberty's eightieth year, we face a fundamental moment in our national and global life. There are no doubt enormous challenges and opportunities to come and some yet to be imagined. Whatever the powerful say about new threats as opposed to old-fashioned values, don't forget the continuing case for our human rights. They were needed by and taken from the victims of the Holocaust. In some parts of the world today, people still only dream of them. They were forged after the Second World War and provided some accountability for, if not always prevention from, grave error, during the War on Terror. Yes they protect criminal suspects; but we can all become suspect sometime. And they protect rape and torture victims too. They protect 'foreigners', but so are we all. Human rights empower the vulnerable and irritate and inconvenience the mighty. But, trust me, you won't know what you had till it's gone.

Changes to legislation: There are outstanding changes not yet made by the legislation.gov.uk
editorial team to Human Rights Act 1998. Any changes that have already been made by the team
appear in the content and are referenced with annotations. (See end of Document for details)

Human Rights Act 1998

1998 CHAPTER 42

An Act to give further effect to rights and freedoms guaranteed under the European Convention on Human Rights; to make provision with respect to holders of certain judicial offices who become judges of the European Court of Human Rights; and for connected purposes. [9th November 1998]

Be it enacted by the Queen's most Excellent Majesty, by and with the advice and consent of the Lords Spiritual and Temporal, and Commons, in this present Parliament assembled, and by the authority of the same, as follows:—

Annotations:

Extent Information
E1 For the extent of this Act outside the U.K., see s. 22(6)(7)

Modifications etc. (not altering text)
C1 Act: certain functions of the Secretary of State transferred to the Lord Chancellor (26.11.2001) by S.I. 2001/3500, arts. 3, 4, **Sch. 1 para. 5**
C2 Act (except ss. 5, 10, 18, 19 and Sch. 4): Functions of the Lord Chancellor transferred to the Secretary of State, and all property, rights and liabilities to which the Lord Chancellor is entitled or subject to in connection with any such function transferred to the Secretary of State for Constitutional Affairs (19.8.2003) by S.I. 2003/1887, art. 4, **Sch. 1**

Introduction

1   The Convention Rights.

(1) In this Act "the Convention rights" means the rights and fundamental freedoms set out in—

    (a)   Articles 2 to 12 and 14 of the Convention,

    (b)   Articles 1 to 3 of the First Protocol, and

    (c)   [F1Article 1 of the Thirteenth Protocol],

Changes to legislation: There are outstanding changes not yet made by the legislation.gov.uk
editorial team to Human Rights Act 1998. Any changes that have already been made by the team
appear in the content and are referenced with annotations. (See end of Document for details)

as read with Articles 16 to 18 of the Convention.

(2) Those Articles are to have effect for the purposes of this Act subject to any designated derogation or reservation (as to which see sections 14 and 15).

(3) The Articles are set out in Schedule 1.

(4) The [F2Secretary of State] may by order make such amendments to this Act as he considers appropriate to reflect the effect, in relation to the United Kingdom, of a protocol.

(5) In subsection (4) "protocol" means a protocol to the Convention—

(a) which the United Kingdom has ratified; or

(b) which the United Kingdom has signed with a view to ratification.

(6) No amendment may be made by an order under subsection (4) so as to come into force before the protocol concerned is in force in relation to the United Kingdom.

Annotations:

Amendments (Textual)

F1 Words in s. 1(1)(c) substituted (22.6.2004) by The Human Rights Act 1998 (Amendment) Order 2004 (S. I. 2004/1574), **art. 2(1)**

F2 Words in s. 1 substituted (19.8.2003) by The Secretary of State for Constitutional Affairs Order 2003 (S. I. 2003/1887), art. 9, **Sch. 2 para. 10(1)**

2   Interpretation of Convention rights.

(1) A court or tribunal determining a question which has arisen in connection with a Convention right must take into account any—

(a) judgment, decision, declaration or advisory opinion of the European Court of Human Rights,

(b) opinion of the Commission given in a report adopted under Article 31 of the Convention,

(c) decision of the Commission in connection with Article 26 or 27(2) of the Convention, or

(d) decision of the Committee of Ministers taken under Article 46 of the Convention,

whenever made or given, so far as, in the opinion of the court or tribunal, it is relevant to the proceedings in which that question has arisen.

(2) Evidence of any judgment, decision, declaration or opinion of which account may have to be taken under this section is to be given in proceedings before any court or tribunal in such manner as may be provided by rules.

(3) In this section "rules" means rules of court or, in the case of proceedings before a tribunal, rules made for the purposes of this section—

(a) by F3 . . . [F4the Lord Chancellor or] the Secretary of State, in relation to any proceedings outside Scotland;

(b) by the Secretary of State, in relation to proceedings in Scotland; or

(c) by a Northern Ireland department, in relation to proceedings before a tribunal in Northern Ireland—

Changes to legislation: There are outstanding changes not yet made by the legislation.gov.uk
editorial team to Human Rights Act 1998. Any changes that have already been made by the team
appear in the content and are referenced with annotations. (See end of Document for details)

(i) which deals with transferred matters; and

(ii) for which no rules made under paragraph (a) are in force.

Annotations:

Amendments (Textual)

F3   Words in s. 2(3)(a) repealed (19.8.2003) by The Secretary of State for Constitutional Affairs Order
2003 (S. I. 2003/1887), art. 9, **Sch. 2 para. 10(2)**

F4   Words in s. 2(3)(a) inserted (12.1.2006) by The Transfer of Functions (Lord Chancellor and Secretary
of State) Order 2005 (S.I. 2005/3429), art. 8, **Sch. para. 3**

Modifications etc. (not altering text)

C3   S. 2(3)(a): functions of the Secretary of State to be exercisable concurrently with the Lord Chancellor
(12.1.2006) by The Transfer of Functions (Lord Chancellor and Secretary of State) Order 2005 (S.I.
2005/3429), **art. 3(2)** (with arts. 4, 5)

Legislation

3   Interpretation of legislation.

(1) So far as it is possible to do so, primary legislation and subordinate legislation must
be read and given effect in a way which is compatible with the Convention rights.

(2) This section—

(a)   applies to primary legislation and subordinate legislation whenever enacted;

(b)   does not affect the validity, continuing operation or enforcement of any
incompatible primary legislation; and

(c)   does not affect the validity, continuing operation or enforcement of any
incompatible subordinate legislation if (disregarding any possibility of
revocation) primary legislation prevents removal of the incompatibility.

4   Declaration of incompatibility.

(1) Subsection (2) applies in any proceedings in which a court determines whether a
provision of primary legislation is compatible with a Convention right.

(2) If the court is satisfied that the provision is incompatible with a Convention right, it
may make a declaration of that incompatibility.

(3) Subsection (4) applies in any proceedings in which a court determines whether a
provision of subordinate legislation, made in the exercise of a power conferred by
primary legislation, is compatible with a Convention right.

(4) If the court is satisfied—

(a)   that the provision is incompatible with a Convention right, and

(b)   that (disregarding any possibility of revocation) the primary legislation
concerned prevents removal of the incompatibility,

it may make a declaration of that incompatibility.

(5) In this section "court" means—

[F5(a)   the Supreme Court;]

Changes to legislation: There are outstanding changes not yet made by the legislation.gov.uk
editorial team to Human Rights Act 1998. Any changes that have already been made by the team
appear in the content and are referenced with annotations. (See end of Document for details)

(b)   the Judicial Committee of the Privy Council;

(c)   the [^{F6}Court Martial Appeal Court] ;

(d)   in Scotland, the High Court of Justiciary sitting otherwise than as a trial court or the Court of Session;

(e)   in England and Wales or Northern Ireland, the High Court or the Court of Appeal.

[^{F7}(f)   the Court of Protection, in any matter being dealt with by the President of the Family Division, the Vice-Chancellor or a puisne judge of the High Court.]

(6) A declaration under this section ("a declaration of incompatibility")—

(a)   does not affect the validity, continuing operation or enforcement of the provision in respect of which it is given; and

(b)   is not binding on the parties to the proceedings in which it is made.

Annotations:

Amendments (Textual)

F5   S. 4(5)(a) substituted (1.10.2009) by Constitutional Reform Act 2005 (c. 4), ss. 40, 148, **Sch. 9 para. 66(2)**; S.I. 2009/1604, **art. 2(d)**

F6   Words in s. 4(5)(c) substituted (28.3.2009 for certain purposes and 31.10.2009 otherwise) by Armed Forces Act 2006 (c. 52), ss. 378, 383, **Sch. 16 para. 156**; S.I. 2009/812, **art. 3** (with transitional provisions in S.I. 2009/1059); S.I. 2009/1167, **art. 4**

F7   S. 4(5)(f) inserted (1.10.2007) by Mental Capacity Act 2005 (c. 9), ss. 67(1), 68(1)-(3), **Sch. 6 para. 43** (with ss. 27, 28, 79, 62); S.I. 2007/1897, **art. 2(1)(c)(d)**

---

5   Right of Crown to intervene.

(1) Where a court is considering whether to make a declaration of incompatibility, the Crown is entitled to notice in accordance with rules of court.

(2) In any case to which subsection (1) applies—

(a)   a Minister of the Crown (or a person nominated by him),

(b)   a member of the Scottish Executive,

(c)   a Northern Ireland Minister,

(d)   a Northern Ireland department,

is entitled, on giving notice in accordance with rules of court, to be joined as a party to the proceedings.

(3) Notice under subsection (2) may be given at any time during the proceedings.

(4) A person who has been made a party to criminal proceedings (other than in Scotland) as the result of a notice under subsection (2) may, with leave, appeal to the [^{F8}Supreme Court] against any declaration of incompatibility made in the proceedings.

(5) In subsection (4)—

"criminal proceedings" includes all proceedings before the [^{F9}Court Martial Appeal Court]; and

"leave" means leave granted by the court making the declaration of incompatibility or by the [^{F10}Supreme Court]

Changes to legislation: *There are outstanding changes not yet made by the legislation.gov.uk editorial team to Human Rights Act 1998. Any changes that have already been made by the team appear in the content and are referenced with annotations. (See end of Document for details)*

Annotations:

Amendments (Textual)

F8   Words in s. 5(4) substituted (1.10.2009) by Constitutional Reform Act 2005 (c. 4), ss. 40, 148, **Sch. 9 para. 66(3)**; S.I. 2009/1604, **art. 2(d)**

F9   Words in s. 5(5) substituted (28.3.2009 for certain purposes and 31.10.2009 otherwise) by Armed Forces Act 2006 (c. 52), ss. 378, 383, **Sch. 16 para. 157**; S.I. 2009/812, **art. 3** (with transitional provisions in S.I. 2009/1059); S.I. 2009/1167, **art. 4**

F10   Words in s. 5(5) substituted (1.10.2009) by Constitutional Reform Act 2005 (c. 4), ss. 40, 148, **Sch. 9 para. 66(3)**; S.I. 2009/1604, **art. 2(d)**

Public authorities

6   **Acts of public authorities.**

(1) It is unlawful for a public authority to act in a way which is incompatible with a Convention right.

(2) Subsection (1) does not apply to an act if—

    (a)   as the result of one or more provisions of primary legislation, the authority could not have acted differently; or

    (b)   in the case of one or more provisions of, or made under, primary legislation which cannot be read or given effect in a way which is compatible with the Convention rights, the authority was acting so as to give effect to or enforce those provisions.

(3) In this section "public authority" includes—

    (a)   a court or tribunal, and

    (b)   any person certain of whose functions are functions of a public nature,

but does not include either House of Parliament or a person exercising functions in connection with proceedings in Parliament.

(4) [F11] . . . .

(5) In relation to a particular act, a person is not a public authority by virtue only of subsection (3)(b) if the nature of the act is private.

(6) "An act" includes a failure to act but does not include a failure to—

    (a)   introduce in, or lay before, Parliament a proposal for legislation; or

    (b)   make any primary legislation or remedial order.

Annotations:

Amendments (Textual)

F11   S. 6(4) repealed (1.10.2009) by Constitutional Reform Act 2005 (c. 4), ss. 40, 146, 148, Sch. 9 para. 66(4), **Sch. 18 Pt. 5**; S.I. 2009/1604, **art. 2(d)(f)**

Modifications etc. (not altering text)

C4   S. 6(1) applied (2.10.2000) by 1999 c. 33, **ss. 65(2)**, 170(4); S.I. 2000/2444, art. 2, **Sch. 1** (subject to transitional provisions in arts. 3, 4, Sch. 2)

Changes to legislation: There are outstanding changes not yet made by the legislation.gov.uk
editorial team to Human Rights Act 1998. Any changes that have already been made by the team
appear in the content and are referenced with annotations. (See end of Document for details)

C5　S. 6(3)(b) modified (1.12.2008 with exception in art. 2(2) of commencing S.I.) by Health and Social
　　Care Act 2008 (c. 14), **ss. 145(1)-(4),** 170 (with s. 145(5)); S.I. 2008/2994, **art. 2(1)**

7　Proceedings.

(1) A person who claims that a public authority has acted (or proposes to act) in a way
which is made unlawful by section 6(1) may—

　(a)　bring proceedings against the authority under this Act in the appropriate court
or tribunal, or

　(b)　rely on the Convention right or rights concerned in any legal proceedings,

but only if he is (or would be) a victim of the unlawful act.

(2) In subsection (1)(a) "appropriate court or tribunal" means such court or tribunal as
may be determined in accordance with rules; and proceedings against an authority
include a counterclaim or similar proceeding.

(3) If the proceedings are brought on an application for judicial review, the applicant is
to be taken to have a sufficient interest in relation to the unlawful act only if he is, or
would be, a victim of that act.

(4) If the proceedings are made by way of a petition for judicial review in Scotland, the
applicant shall be taken to have title and interest to sue in relation to the unlawful act
only if he is, or would be, a victim of that act.

(5) Proceedings under subsection (1)(a) must be brought before the end of—

　(a)　the period of one year beginning with the date on which the act complained
of took place; or

　(b)　such longer period as the court or tribunal considers equitable having regard
to all the circumstances,

but that is subject to any rule imposing a stricter time limit in relation to the procedure
in question.

(6) In subsection (1)(b) "legal proceedings" includes—

　(a)　proceedings brought by or at the instigation of a public authority; and

　(b)　an appeal against the decision of a court or tribunal.

(7) For the purposes of this section, a person is a victim of an unlawful act only if he
would be a victim for the purposes of Article 34 of the Convention if proceedings were
brought in the European Court of Human Rights in respect of that act.

(8) Nothing in this Act creates a criminal offence.

(9) In this section "rules" means—

　(a)　in relation to proceedings before a court or tribunal outside Scotland, rules
made by [F12] . . . [F13the Lord Chancellor or] the Secretary of State for the
purposes of this section or rules of court,

　(b)　in relation to proceedings before a court or tribunal in Scotland, rules made
by the Secretary of State for those purposes,

　(c)　in relation to proceedings before a tribunal in Northern Ireland—

　　　(i)　which deals with transferred matters; and

　　　(ii)　for which no rules made under paragraph (a) are in force,

　　rules made by a Northern Ireland department for those purposes, and includes provision made by order under section 1 of the [M1]Courts and Legal Services Act 1990.

(10) In making rules, regard must be had to section 9.

(11) The Minister who has power to make rules in relation to a particular tribunal may, to the extent he considers it necessary to ensure that the tribunal can provide an appropriate remedy in relation to an act (or proposed act) of a public authority which is (or would be) unlawful as a result of section 6(1), by order add to—

    (a)   the relief or remedies which the tribunal may grant; or

    (b)   the grounds on which it may grant any of them.

(12) An order made under subsection (11) may contain such incidental, supplemental, consequential or transitional provision as the Minister making it considers appropriate.

(13) "The Minister" includes the Northern Ireland department concerned.

Annotations:

Amendments (Textual)

F12   Words in s. 7(9)(a) repealed (19.8.2003) by The Secretary of State for Constitutional Affairs Order 2003 (S. I. 2003/1887), art. 9, **Sch. 2 para. 10(2)**

F13   Words in s. 7(9)(a) inserted (12.1.2006) by The Transfer of Functions (Lord Chancellor and Secretary of State) Order 2005 (S.I. 2005/3429), art. 8, **Sch. para. 3,**

Modifications etc. (not altering text)

C6   S. 7 amended (2.10.2000) by Regulation of Investigatory Powers Act 2000 (c. 23), **ss. 65(2)(a),** 83 (with s. 82(3); S.I. 2000/2543, **art. 3**

C7   S. 7: referred to (11.3.2005) by Prevention of Terrorism Act 2005 (c. 2), {s. 11(2)}

C8   S. 7(9)(a): functions of the Secretary of State to be exercisable concurrently with the Lord Chancellor (12.1.2006) by The Transfer of Functions (Lord Chancellor and Secretary of State) Order 2005 (S.I. 2005/3429), **art. 3(2)** (with arts. 4, 5)

C9   S. 7(11): functions of the Secretary of State to be exercisable concurrently with the Lord Chancellor (12.1.2006) by The Transfer of Functions (Lord Chancellor and Secretary of State) Order 2005 (S.I. 2005/3429), **art. 3(2)** (with arts. 4, 5)

Marginal Citations

M1   1990 c. 41.

8   Judicial remedies.

(1) In relation to any act (or proposed act) of a public authority which the court finds is (or would be) unlawful, it may grant such relief or remedy, or make such order, within its powers as it considers just and appropriate.

(2) But damages may be awarded only by a court which has power to award damages, or to order the payment of compensation, in civil proceedings.

(3) No award of damages is to be made unless, taking account of all the circumstances of the case, including—

    (a)   any other relief or remedy granted, or order made, in relation to the act in question (by that or any other court), and

Changes to legislation: There are outstanding changes not yet made by the legislation.gov.uk
editorial team to Human Rights Act 1998. Any changes that have already been made by the team
appear in the content and are referenced with annotations. (See end of Document for details)

(b)   the consequences of any decision (of that or any other court) in respect of that act,

the court is satisfied that the award is necessary to afford just satisfaction to the person in whose favour it is made.

(4) In determining—

    (a)   whether to award damages, or

    (b)   the amount of an award,

the court must take into account the principles applied by the European Court of Human Rights in relation to the award of compensation under Article 41 of the Convention.

(5) A public authority against which damages are awarded is to be treated—

    (a)   in Scotland, for the purposes of section 3 of the ^{M2}Law Reform (Miscellaneous Provisions) (Scotland) Act 1940 as if the award were made in an action of damages in which the authority has been found liable in respect of loss or damage to the person to whom the award is made;

    (b)   for the purposes of the ^{M3}Civil Liability (Contribution) Act 1978 as liable in respect of damage suffered by the person to whom the award is made.

(6) In this section—

    "court" includes a tribunal;

    "damages" means damages for an unlawful act of a public authority; and

    "unlawful" means unlawful under section 6(1).

Annotations:

Marginal Citations

  M2   1940 c. 42.

  M3   1978 c. 47.

---

9   Judicial acts.

(1) Proceedings under section 7(1)(a) in respect of a judicial act may be brought only—

    (a)   by exercising a right of appeal;

    (b)   on an application (in Scotland a petition) for judicial review; or

    (c)   in such other forum as may be prescribed by rules.

(2) That does not affect any rule of law which prevents a court from being the subject of judicial review.

(3) In proceedings under this Act in respect of a judicial act done in good faith, damages may not be awarded otherwise than to compensate a person to the extent required by Article 5(5) of the Convention.

(4) An award of damages permitted by subsection (3) is to be made against the Crown; but no award may be made unless the appropriate person, if not a party to the proceedings, is joined.

(5) In this section—

    "appropriate person" means the Minister responsible for the court concerned, or a person or government department nominated by him;

Human Rights Act 1998 (c. 42)
Document Generated: 2014-07-03

Changes to legislation: There are outstanding changes not yet made by the legislation.gov.uk
editorial team to Human Rights Act 1998. Any changes that have already been made by the team
appear in the content and are referenced with annotations. (See end of Document for details)

"court" includes a tribunal;

"judge" includes a member of a tribunal, a justice of the peace [F14(or, in Northern Ireland, a lay magistrate)] and a clerk or other officer entitled to exercise the jurisdiction of a court;

"judicial act" means a judicial act of a court and includes an act done on the instructions, or on behalf, of a judge; and

"rules" has the same meaning as in section 7(9).

Annotations:

Amendments (Textual)

F14 Words in definition s. 9(5) inserted (N.I.)(1.4.2005) by 2002 c. 26, s. 10(6), Sch. 4 para. 39; S.R. 2005/109, **art. 2** Sch.

Remedial action

10   **Power to take remedial action.**

(1) This section applies if—

   (a) a provision of legislation has been declared under section 4 to be incompatible with a Convention right and, if an appeal lies—

      (i) all persons who may appeal have stated in writing that they do not intend to do so;

      (ii) the time for bringing an appeal has expired and no appeal has been brought within that time; or

      (iii) an appeal brought within that time has been determined or abandoned; or

   (b) it appears to a Minister of the Crown or Her Majesty in Council that, having regard to a finding of the European Court of Human Rights made after the coming into force of this section in proceedings against the United Kingdom, a provision of legislation is incompatible with an obligation of the United Kingdom arising from the Convention.

(2) If a Minister of the Crown considers that there are compelling reasons for proceeding under this section, he may by order make such amendments to the legislation as he considers necessary to remove the incompatibility.

(3) If, in the case of subordinate legislation, a Minister of the Crown considers—

   (a) that it is necessary to amend the primary legislation under which the subordinate legislation in question was made, in order to enable the incompatibility to be removed, and

   (b) that there are compelling reasons for proceeding under this section,

he may by order make such amendments to the primary legislation as he considers necessary.

(4) This section also applies where the provision in question is in subordinate legislation and has been quashed, or declared invalid, by reason of incompatibility with a Convention right and the Minister proposes to proceed under paragraph 2(b) of Schedule 2.

*Changes to legislation: There are outstanding changes not yet made by the legislation.gov.uk
editorial team to Human Rights Act 1998. Any changes that have already been made by the team
appear in the content and are referenced with annotations. (See end of Document for details)*

(5) If the legislation is an Order in Council, the power conferred by subsection (2) or (3) is exercisable by Her Majesty in Council.

(6) In this section "legislation" does not include a Measure of the Church Assembly or of the General Synod of the Church of England.

(7) Schedule 2 makes further provision about remedial orders.

Other rights and proceedings

11   Safeguard for existing human rights.

A person's reliance on a Convention right does not restrict—
    (a)   any other right or freedom conferred on him by or under any law having effect in any part of the United Kingdom; or
    (b)   his right to make any claim or bring any proceedings which he could make or bring apart from sections 7 to 9.

12   Freedom of expression.

(1) This section applies if a court is considering whether to grant any relief which, if granted, might affect the exercise of the Convention right to freedom of expression.

(2) If the person against whom the application for relief is made ("the respondent") is neither present nor represented, no such relief is to be granted unless the court is satisfied—
    (a)   that the applicant has taken all practicable steps to notify the respondent; or
    (b)   that there are compelling reasons why the respondent should not be notified.

(3) No such relief is to be granted so as to restrain publication before trial unless the court is satisfied that the applicant is likely to establish that publication should not be allowed.

(4) The court must have particular regard to the importance of the Convention right to freedom of expression and, where the proceedings relate to material which the respondent claims, or which appears to the court, to be journalistic, literary or artistic material (or to conduct connected with such material), to—
    (a)   the extent to which—
        (i) the material has, or is about to, become available to the public; or
        (ii) it is, or would be, in the public interest for the material to be published;
    (b)   any relevant privacy code.

(5) In this section—
    "court" includes a tribunal; and
    "relief" includes any remedy or order (other than in criminal proceedings).

13   Freedom of thought, conscience and religion.

(1) If a court's determination of any question arising under this Act might affect the exercise by a religious organisation (itself or its members collectively) of the

Changes to legislation: There are outstanding changes not yet made by the legislation.gov.uk
editorial team to Human Rights Act 1998. Any changes that have already been made by the team
appear in the content and are referenced with annotations. (See end of Document for details)

Convention right to freedom of thought, conscience and religion, it must have
particular regard to the importance of that right.

(2) In this section "court" includes a tribunal.

Derogations and reservations

14   Derogations.

(1) In this Act "designated derogation" means—
     F15
     . . . .
     any derogation by the United Kingdom from an Article of the Convention, or of
     any protocol to the Convention, which is designated for the purposes of this Act
     in an order made by the [F16Secretary of State]

F17(2) . . . ./. . . .

(3) If a designated derogation is amended or replaced it ceases to be a designated
derogation.

(4) But subsection (3) does not prevent the [F18Secretary of State] from exercising his
power under subsection (1) F19. . . to make a fresh designation order in respect of the
Article concerned.

(5) The [F20Secretary of State] must by order make such amendments to Schedule 3 as he
considers appropriate to reflect—
     (a)   any designation order; or
     (b)   the effect of subsection (3).

(6) A designation order may be made in anticipation of the making by the United Kingdom
of a proposed derogation.

Annotations:

Amendments (Textual)

F15   S. 14(1): from "(a)" to "(b)" repealed (1.4.2001) by S.I. 2001/1216, **art. 2(a)**

F16   Words in s. 14 substituted (19.8.2003) by The Secretary of State for Constitutional Affairs Order 2003
          (S. I. 2003/1887), art. 9, **Sch. 2 para. 10(1)**

F17   S. 14(2) repealed (1.4.2001) by S.I. 2001/1216, **art. 2(b)**

F18   Words in s. 14 substituted (19.8.2003) by The Secretary of State for Constitutional Affairs Order 2003
          (S. I. 2003/1887), art. 9, **Sch. 2 para. 10(1)**

F19   S. 14(4): "(b)" repealed (1.4.2001) by S.I. 2001/1216, **art. 2(c)**

F20   Words in s. 14 substituted (19.8.2003) by The Secretary of State for Constitutional Affairs Order 2003
          (S. I. 2003/1887), art. 9, **Sch. 2 para. 10(1)**

---

15   Reservations.

(1) In this Act "designated reservation" means—
     (a)   the United Kingdom's reservation to Article 2 of the First Protocol to the
            Convention; and

    (b)   any other reservation by the United Kingdom to an Article of the Convention, or of any protocol to the Convention, which is designated for the purposes of this Act in an order made by the [F21Secretary of State] .

(2) The text of the reservation referred to in subsection (1)(a) is set out in Part II of Schedule 3.

(3) If a designated reservation is withdrawn wholly or in part it ceases to be a designated reservation.

(4) But subsection (3) does not prevent the [F22Secretary of State] from exercising his power under subsection (1)(b) to make a fresh designation order in respect of the Article concerned.

(5) [F23Secretary of State] must by order make such amendments to this Act as he considers appropriate to reflect—

    (a)   any designation order; or

    (b)   the effect of subsection (3).

Annotations:

Amendments (Textual)

F21 Words in s. 15 substituted (19.8.2003) by The Secretary of State for Constitutional Affairs Order 2003 (S. I. 2003/1887), art. 9, **Sch. 2 para. 10(1)**

F22 Words in s. 15 substituted (19.8.2003) by The Secretary of State for Constitutional Affairs Order 2003 (S. I. 2003/1887), art. 9, **Sch. 2 para. 10(1)**

F23 Words in s. 15 substituted (19.8.2003) by The Secretary of State for Constitutional Affairs Order 2003 (S. I. 2003/1887), art. 9, **Sch. 2 para. 10(1)**

---

16   **Period for which designated derogations have effect.**

(1) If it has not already been withdrawn by the United Kingdom, a designated derogation ceases to have effect for the purposes of this Act—

F24
. . . .

. . ., at the end of the period of five years beginning with the date on which the order designating it was made.

(2) At any time before the period—

    (a)   fixed by subsection (1) F25. . ., or

    (b)   extended by an order under this subsection,

comes to an end, the [F26Secretary of State] may by order extend it by a further period of five years.

(3) An order under section 14(1) F27. . . ceases to have effect at the end of the period for consideration, unless a resolution has been passed by each House approving the order.

(4) Subsection (3) does not affect—

    (a)   anything done in reliance on the order; or

    (b)   the power to make a fresh order under section 14(1) . . ..

(5) In subsection (3) "period for consideration" means the period of forty days beginning with the day on which the order was made.

Changes to legislation: There are outstanding changes not yet made by the legislation.gov.uk
editorial team to Human Rights Act 1998. Any changes that have already been made by the team
appear in the content and are referenced with annotations. (See end of Document for details)

(6) In calculating the period for consideration, no account is to be taken of any time during which—

    (a)   Parliament is dissolved or prorogued; or

    (b)   both Houses are adjourned for more than four days.

(7) If a designated derogation is withdrawn by the United Kingdom, the [F28Secretary of State] must by order make such amendments to this Act as he considers are required to reflect that withdrawal.

Annotations:

Amendments (Textual)

F24   S. 16(1): words from "(a)" to "any other derogation" repealed (1.4.2001) by S.I. 2001/1216, **art. 3(a)**

F25   Words in s. 16(2)(a) repealed (1.4.2001) by S.I. 2001/1216, **art. 3(b)**

F26   Words in s. 16 substituted (19.8.2003) by The Secretary of State for Constitutional Affairs Order 2003 (S. I. 2003/1887), art. 9, **Sch. 2 para. 10(1)**

F27   S. 16(3)(4)(b): "(b)" repealed (1.4.2001) by S.I. 2001/1216, **art. 3(c)(d)**

F28   Words in s. 16 substituted (19.8.2003) by The Secretary of State for Constitutional Affairs Order 2003 (S. I. 2003/1887), art. 9, **Sch. 2 para. 10(1)**

17   **Periodic review of designated reservations.**

(1) The appropriate Minister must review the designated reservation referred to in section 15(1)(a)—

    (a)   before the end of the period of five years beginning with the date on which section 1(2) came into force; and

    (b)   if that designation is still in force, before the end of the period of five years beginning with the date on which the last report relating to it was laid under subsection (3).

(2) The appropriate Minister must review each of the other designated reservations (if any)—

    (a)   before the end of the period of five years beginning with the date on which the order designating the reservation first came into force; and

    (b)   if the designation is still in force, before the end of the period of five years beginning with the date on which the last report relating to it was laid under subsection (3).

(3) The Minister conducting a review under this section must prepare a report on the result of the review and lay a copy of it before each House of Parliament.

Judges of the European Court of Human Rights

18   **Appointment to European Court of Human Rights.**

(1) In this section "judicial office" means the office of—

    (a)   Lord Justice of Appeal, Justice of the High Court or Circuit judge, in England and Wales;

    (b)   judge of the Court of Session or sheriff, in Scotland;

Human Rights Act 1998 (c. 42)
Document Generated: 2014-07-03

Changes to legislation: *There are outstanding changes not yet made by the legislation.gov.uk editorial team to Human Rights Act 1998. Any changes that have already been made by the team appear in the content and are referenced with annotations. (See end of Document for details)*

(c) Lord Justice of Appeal, judge of the High Court or county court judge, in Northern Ireland.

(2) The holder of a judicial office may become a judge of the European Court of Human Rights ("the Court") without being required to relinquish his office.

(3) But he is not required to perform the duties of his judicial office while he is a judge of the Court.

(4) In respect of any period during which he is a judge of the Court—

(a) a Lord Justice of Appeal or Justice of the High Court is not to count as a judge of the relevant court for the purposes of section 2(1) or 4(1) of the [F29Senior Courts Act 1981](maximum number of judges) nor as a judge of the [F30Senior Courts] for the purposes of section 12(1) to (6) of that Act (salaries etc.);

(b) a judge of the Court of Session is not to count as a judge of that court for the purposes of section 1(1) of the M4Court of Session Act 1988 (maximum number of judges) or of section 9(1)(c) of the M5Administration of Justice Act 1973 ("the 1973 Act") (salaries etc.);

(c) a Lord Justice of Appeal or judge of the High Court in Northern Ireland is not to count as a judge of the relevant court for the purposes of section 2(1) or 3(1) of the M6Judicature (Northern Ireland) Act 1978 (maximum number of judges) nor as a judge of the [F31Court of Judicature] of Northern Ireland for the purposes of section 9(1)(d) of the 1973 Act (salaries etc.);

(d) a Circuit judge is not to count as such for the purposes of section 18 of the M7Courts Act 1971 (salaries etc.);

(e) a sheriff is not to count as such for the purposes of section 14 of the M8Sheriff Courts (Scotland) Act 1907 (salaries etc.);

(f) a county court judge of Northern Ireland is not to count as such for the purposes of section 106 of the M9County Courts Act Northern Ireland) 1959 (salaries etc.).

(5) If a sheriff principal is appointed a judge of the Court, section 11(1) of the M10Sheriff Courts (Scotland) Act 1971 (temporary appointment of sheriff principal) applies, while he holds that appointment, as if his office is vacant.

(6) Schedule 4 makes provision about judicial pensions in relation to the holder of a judicial office who serves as a judge of the Court.

(7) The Lord Chancellor or the Secretary of State may by order make such transitional provision (including, in particular, provision for a temporary increase in the maximum number of judges) as he considers appropriate in relation to any holder of a judicial office who has completed his service as a judge of the Court.

[F32(7A) The following paragraphs apply to the making of an order under subsection (7) in relation to any holder of a judicial office listed in subsection (1)(a)—

(a) before deciding what transitional provision it is appropriate to make, the person making the order must consult the Lord Chief Justice of England and Wales;

(b) before making the order, that person must consult the Lord Chief Justice of England and Wales.

(7B) The following paragraphs apply to the making of an order under subsection (7) in relation to any holder of a judicial office listed in subsection (1)(c)—

 (a) before deciding what transitional provision it is appropriate to make, the person making the order must consult the Lord Chief Justice of Northern Ireland;

 (b) before making the order, that person must consult the Lord Chief Justice of Northern Ireland.

(7C) The Lord Chief Justice of England and Wales may nominate a judicial office holder (within the meaning of section 109(4) of the Constitutional Reform Act 2005) to exercise his functions under this section.

(7D) The Lord Chief Justice of Northern Ireland may nominate any of the following to exercise his functions under this section—

 (a) the holder of one of the offices listed in Schedule 1 to the Justice (Northern Ireland) Act 2002;

 (b) a Lord Justice of Appeal (as defined in section 88 of that Act).]

Annotations:

Amendments (Textual)

F29 Words in s. 18(4)(a) substituted (1.10.2009) by Constitutional Reform Act 2005 (c. 4), ss. 59, 148, Sch. 11 para. 4; S.I. 2009/1604, art. 2(d)

F30 Words in s. 18(4)(a) substituted (1.10.2009) by Constitutional Reform Act 2005 (c. 4), ss. 59, 148, Sch. 11 para. 4; S.I. 2009/1604, art. 2(d)

F31 Words in s. 18(4)(c) substituted (1.10.2009) by Constitutional Reform Act 2005 (c. 4), ss. 59, 148, Sch. 11 para. 6; S.I. 2009/1604, art. 2(d)

F32 S. 18(7A)-(7D) inserted (3.4.2006) by Constitutional Reform Act 2005 (c. 4), ss. 15, 148, Sch. 4 para. 278; S.I. 2006/1014, art. 2, Sch. 1 para. 11(v)

Marginal Citations

M4 1988 c. 36.
M5 1973 c. 15.
M6 1978 c. 23.
M7 1971 c. 23
M8 1907 c. 51.
M9 1959 c. 25 (N.I.).
M10 1971 c. 58.

Parliamentary procedure

19 **Statements of compatibility.**

(1) A Minister of the Crown in charge of a Bill in either House of Parliament must, before Second Reading of the Bill—

 (a) make a statement to the effect that in his view the provisions of the Bill are compatible with the Convention rights ("a statement of compatibility"); or

 (b) make a statement to the effect that although he is unable to make a statement of compatibility the government nevertheless wishes the House to proceed with the Bill.

(2) The statement must be in writing and be published in such manner as the Minister making it considers appropriate.

Changes to legislation: There are outstanding changes not yet made by the legislation.gov.uk
editorial team to Human Rights Act 1998. Any changes that have already been made by the team
appear in the content and are referenced with annotations. (See end of Document for details)

Supplemental

20   Orders etc. under this Act.

(1) Any power of a Minister of the Crown to make an order under this Act is exercisable by statutory instrument.

(2) The power of ^{F33} . . . [^{F34}the Lord Chancellor or] the Secretary of State to make rules (other than rules of court) under section 2(3) or 7(9) is exercisable by statutory instrument.

(3) Any statutory instrument made under section 14, 15 or 16(7) must be laid before Parliament.

(4) No order may be made by ^{F35} . . . [^{F36}the Lord Chancellor or] the Secretary of State under section 1(4), 7(11) or 16(2) unless a draft of the order has been laid before, and approved by, each House of Parliament.

(5) Any statutory instrument made under section 18(7) or Schedule 4, or to which subsection (2) applies, shall be subject to annulment in pursuance of a resolution of either House of Parliament.

(6) The power of a Northern Ireland department to make—

(a)   rules under section 2(3)(c) or 7(9)(c), or

(b)   an order under section 7(11),

is exercisable by statutory rule for the purposes of the ^{M11}Statutory Rules (Northern Ireland) Order 1979.

(7) Any rules made under section 2(3)(c) or 7(9)(c) shall be subject to negative resolution; and section 41(6) of the ^{M12}Interpretation Act Northern Ireland) 1954 (meaning of "subject to negative resolution") shall apply as if the power to make the rules were conferred by an Act of the Northern Ireland Assembly.

(8) No order may be made by a Northern Ireland department under section 7(11) unless a draft of the order has been laid before, and approved by, the Northern Ireland Assembly.

Annotations:

Amendments (Textual)

F33   Words in s. 20(2) repealed (19.8.2003) by The Secretary of State for Constitutional Affairs Order 2003 (S. I. 2003/1887), art. 9, **Sch. 2 para. 10(2)**

F34   Words in s. 20(2) inserted (12.1.2006) by The Transfer of Functions (Lord Chancellor and Secretary of State) Order 2005 (S.I. 2005/3429), art. 8, **Sch. para. 3**

F35   Words in s. 20(4) repealed (19.8.2003) by The Secretary of State for Constitutional Affairs Order 2003 (S. I. 2003/1887), art. 9, **Sch. 2 para. 10(2)**

F36   Words in s. 20(4) inserted (12.1.2006) by The Transfer of Functions (Lord Chancellor and Secretary of State) Order 2005 (S.I. 2005/3429), art. 8, **Sch. para. 3**

Marginal Citations

M11   S.I. 1979/1573 (N.I. 12).

M12   1954 c. 33 (N.I.).

*Changes to legislation: There are outstanding changes not yet made by the legislation.gov.uk
editorial team to Human Rights Act 1998. Any changes that have already been made by the team
appear in the content and are referenced with annotations. (See end of Document for details)*

21   Interpretation, etc.

(1) In this Act—

"amend" includes repeal and apply (with or without modifications);

"the appropriate Minister" means the Minister of the Crown having charge of the appropriate authorised government department (within the meaning of the [M13]Crown Proceedings Act 1947);

"the Commission" means the European Commission of Human Rights;

"the Convention" means the Convention for the Protection of Human Rights and Fundamental Freedoms, agreed by the Council of Europe at Rome on 4th November 1950 as it has effect for the time being in relation to the United Kingdom;

"declaration of incompatibility" means a declaration under section 4;

"Minister of the Crown" has the same meaning as in the Ministers of the [M14]Crown Act 1975;

"Northern Ireland Minister" includes the First Minister and the deputy First Minister in Northern Ireland;

"primary legislation" means any—

(a) public general Act;

(b) local and personal Act;

(c) private Act;

(d) Measure of the Church Assembly;

(e) Measure of the General Synod of the Church of England;

(f) Order in Council—

(i) made in exercise of Her Majesty's Royal Prerogative;

(ii) made under section 38(1)(a) of the [M15]Northern Ireland Constitution Act 1973 or the corresponding provision of the Northern Ireland Act 1998; or

(iii) amending an Act of a kind mentioned in paragraph (a), (b) or (c);

and includes an order or other instrument made under primary legislation (otherwise than by the [F37Welsh Ministers, the First Minister for Wales, the Counsel General to the Welsh Assembly Government,] a member of the Scottish Executive, a Northern Ireland Minister or a Northern Ireland department) to the extent to which it operates to bring one or more provisions of that legislation into force or amends any primary legislation;

"the First Protocol" means the protocol to the Convention agreed at Paris on 20th March 1952;

[F38] . . .

"the Eleventh Protocol" means the protocol to the Convention (restructuring the control machinery established by the Convention) agreed at Strasbourg on 11th May 1994;

[F39"the Thirteenth Protocol" means the protocol to the Convention (concerning the abolition of the death penalty in all circumstances) agreed at Vilnius on 3rd May 2002;]

"remedial order" means an order under section 10;

"subordinate legislation" means any—

(a) Order in Council other than one—

(i) made in exercise of Her Majesty's Royal Prerogative;

Human Rights Act 1998 (c. 42)
Document Generated: 2014-07-03

*Changes to legislation: There are outstanding changes not yet made by the legislation.gov.uk
editorial team to Human Rights Act 1998. Any changes that have already been made by the team
appear in the content and are referenced with annotations. (See end of Document for details)*

    (ii) made under section 38(1)(a) of the Northern Ireland Constitution Act 1973 or the corresponding provision of the Northern Ireland Act 1998; or

    (iii) amending an Act of a kind mentioned in the definition of primary legislation;

  (b) Act of the Scottish Parliament;

  (ba) [^F40^Measure of the National Assembly for Wales;

  (bb) Act of the National Assembly for Wales;]

  (c) Act of the Parliament of Northern Ireland;

  (d) Measure of the Assembly established under section 1 of the ^M16^Northern Ireland Assembly Act 1973;

  (e) Act of the Northern Ireland Assembly;

  (f) order, rules, regulations, scheme, warrant, byelaw or other instrument made under primary legislation (except to the extent to which it operates to bring one or more provisions of that legislation into force or amends any primary legislation);

  (g) order, rules, regulations, scheme, warrant, byelaw or other instrument made under legislation mentioned in paragraph (b), (c), (d) or (e) or made under an Order in Council applying only to Northern Ireland;

  (h) order, rules, regulations, scheme, warrant, byelaw or other instrument made by a member of the Scottish Executive [^F41^, Welsh Ministers, the First Minister for Wales, the Counsel General to the Welsh Assembly Government,] a Northern Ireland Minister or a Northern Ireland department in exercise of prerogative or other executive functions of Her Majesty which are exercisable by such a person on behalf of Her Majesty;

"transferred matters" has the same meaning as in the Northern Ireland Act 1998; and

"tribunal" means any tribunal in which legal proceedings may be brought.

(2) The references in paragraphs (b) and (c) of section 2(1) to Articles are to Articles of the Convention as they had effect immediately before the coming into force of the Eleventh Protocol.

(3) The reference in paragraph (d) of section 2(1) to Article 46 includes a reference to Articles 32 and 54 of the Convention as they had effect immediately before the coming into force of the Eleventh Protocol.

(4) The references in section 2(1) to a report or decision of the Commission or a decision of the Committee of Ministers include references to a report or decision made as provided by paragraphs 3, 4 and 6 of Article 5 of the Eleventh Protocol (transitional provisions).

(5) ^F42^ . . . .

Annotations:

Extent Information

E2   For the extent of s. 21 outside the U.K. see s. 22(7)

Amendments (Textual)

F37   Words in the definition of "primary legislation" in s. 21(1) substituted by Government of Wales Act 2006 (c. 32), s. 160(1), **Sch. 10 para.56(2)** (with Sch. 11 para. 22) the amending provision coming into force immediately after "the 2007 election" (held on 3.5.2007) subject to s. 161(4)(5) of the amending

Changes to legislation: There are outstanding changes not yet made by the legislation.gov.uk
editorial team to Human Rights Act 1998. Any changes that have already been made by the team
appear in the content and are referenced with annotations. (See end of Document for details)

Act, which provides for certain provisions to come into force for specified purposes immediately after the end of "the initial period" (which ended with the day of the first appointment of a First Minister on 25.5.2007) - see ss. 46, 161(1)(4)(5) of the amending Act.

F38 S. 21(1): definition of "the Sixth Protocol" omitted (22.6.2004) by virtue of The Human Rights Act 1998 (Amendment) Order 2004 (S.I. 2004/1574), **art. 2(2)**

F39 S. 21(1): definition of "the Thirteenth Protocol" inserted (22.6.2004) by virtue of The Human Rights Act 1998 (Amendment) Order 2004 (S.I. 2004/1574), **art. 2(2)**

F40 Words in the definition of "subordinate legislation" in s. 21(1) substituted by Government of Wales Act 2006 (c. 32), s. 160(1), **Sch. 10 para.56(3)** (with Sch. 11 para 22) the amending provision coming into force immediately after "the 2007 election" (held on 3.5.2007) subject to s. 161(4)(5) of the amending Act, which provides for certain provisions to come into force for specified purposes immediately after the end of "the initial period" (which ended with the day of the first appointment of a First Minister on 25.5.2007) - see ss. 46, 161(1)(4)(5) of the amending Act.

F41 Words in the definition of "subordinate legislation" in s. 21(1) substituted by Government of Wales Act 2006 (c. 32), s. 160(1), **Sch. 10 para.56(4)** (with Sch. 11 para. 22) the amending provision coming into force immediately after "the 2007 election" (held on 3.5.2007) subject to s. 161(4)(5) of the amending Act, which provides for certain provisions to come into force for specified purposes immediately after the end of "the initial period" (which ended with the day of the first appointment of a First Minister on 25.5.2007) - see ss. 46, 161(1)(4)(5) of the amending Act.

F42 S. 21(5) repealed (28.3.2009 for certain purposes and 31.10.2009 otherwise) by Armed Forces Act 2006 (c. 52), ss. 378, 383, Sch. 17; S.I. 2009/812, art. 3 (with transitional provisions in S.I. 2009/1059); S.I. 2009/1167, art. 4

Commencement Information

I1 S. 21 wholly in force at 2.10.2000; s. 21(5) in force at Royal Assent, see s. 22(2)(3); s. 21 in force so far as not already in force (2.10.2000) by S.I. 2000/1851, **art. 2**

Marginal Citations

M13 1947 c. 44.
M14 1975 c. 26.
M15 1973 c. 36.
M16 1973 c. 17.

22 Short title, commencement, application and extent.

(1) This Act may be cited as the Human Rights Act 1998.

(2) Sections 18, 20 and 21(5) and this section come into force on the passing of this Act.

(3) The other provisions of this Act come into force on such day as the Secretary of State may by order appoint; and different days may be appointed for different purposes.

(4) Paragraph (b) of subsection (1) of section 7 applies to proceedings brought by or at the instigation of a public authority whenever the act in question took place; but otherwise that subsection does not apply to an act taking place before the coming into force of that section.

(5) This Act binds the Crown.

(6) This Act extends to Northern Ireland.

(7) **F43** . . . .

*Changes to legislation: There are outstanding changes not yet made by the legislation.gov.uk
editorial team to Human Rights Act 1998. Any changes that have already been made by the team
appear in the content and are referenced with annotations. (See end of Document for details)*

Annotations:

Subordinate Legislation Made

P1   S. 22(3) power partly exercised: 24.11.1998 appointed for specified provisions by S.I. 1998/2882, **art. 2**

S. 22(3) power fully exercised: 2.10.2000 appointed for remaining provisions by S.I. 2000/1851, **art. 2**

Amendments (Textual)

F43   S. 22(7) repealed (28.3.2009 for certain purposes and 31.10.2009 otherwise) by Armed Forces Act 2006 (c. 52), ss. 378, 383, **Sch. 17**; S.I. 2009/812, **art. 3** (with transitional provisions in S.I. 2009/1059); S.I. 2009/1167, **art. 4**

Changes to legislation: *There are outstanding changes not yet made by the legislation.gov.uk*
editorial team to Human Rights Act 1998. Any changes that have already been made by the team
appear in the content and are referenced with annotations. (See end of Document for details)

SCHEDULES

SCHEDULE 1

Section 1(3).

THE ARTICLES

PART I

THE CONVENTION

RIGHTS AND FREEDOMS

ARTICLE 2

RIGHT TO LIFE

1   Everyone's right to life shall be protected by law. No one shall be deprived of his life intentionally save in the execution of a sentence of a court following his conviction of a crime for which this penalty is provided by law.

2   Deprivation of life shall not be regarded as inflicted in contravention of this Article when it results from the use of force which is no more than absolutely necessary:

   (a)   in defence of any person from unlawful violence;
   (b)   in order to effect a lawful arrest or to prevent the escape of a person lawfully detained;
   (c)   in action lawfully taken for the purpose of quelling a riot or insurrection.

ARTICLE 3

PROHIBITION OF TORTURE

No one shall be subjected to torture or to inhuman or degrading treatment or punishment.

ARTICLE 4

PROHIBITION OF SLAVERY AND FORCED LABOUR

1   No one shall be held in slavery or servitude.

2   No one shall be required to perform forced or compulsory labour.

3   For the purpose of this Article the term "forced or compulsory labour" shall not include:

   (a)   any work required to be done in the ordinary course of detention imposed according to the provisions of Article 5 of this Convention or during conditional release from such detention;

Human Rights Act 1998 (c. 42)
SCHEDULE 1 – The Articles
Document Generated: 2014-07-03

*Changes to legislation: There are outstanding changes not yet made by the legislation.gov.uk
editorial team to Human Rights Act 1998. Any changes that have already been made by the team
appear in the content and are referenced with annotations. (See end of Document for details)*

(b)   any service of a military character or, in case of conscientious objectors in countries where they are recognised, service exacted instead of compulsory military service;

(c)   any service exacted in case of an emergency or calamity threatening the life or well-being of the community;

(d)   any work or service which forms part of normal civic obligations.

ARTICLE 5

RIGHT TO LIBERTY AND SECURITY

1   Everyone has the right to liberty and security of person. No one shall be deprived of his liberty save in the following cases and in accordance with a procedure prescribed by law:

(a)   the lawful detention of a person after conviction by a competent court;

(b)   the lawful arrest or detention of a person for non-compliance with the lawful order of a court or in order to secure the fulfilment of any obligation prescribed by law;

(c)   the lawful arrest or detention of a person effected for the purpose of bringing him before the competent legal authority on reasonable suspicion of having committed an offence or when it is reasonably considered necessary to prevent his committing an offence or fleeing after having done so;

(d)   the detention of a minor by lawful order for the purpose of educational supervision or his lawful detention for the purpose of bringing him before the competent legal authority;

(e)   the lawful detention of persons for the prevention of the spreading of infectious diseases, of persons of unsound mind, alcoholics or drug addicts or vagrants;

(f)   the lawful arrest or detention of a person to prevent his effecting an unauthorised entry into the country or of a person against whom action is being taken with a view to deportation or extradition.

2   Everyone who is arrested shall be informed promptly, in a language which he understands, of the reasons for his arrest and of any charge against him.

3   Everyone arrested or detained in accordance with the provisions of paragraph 1(c) of this Article shall be brought promptly before a judge or other officer authorised by law to exercise judicial power and shall be entitled to trial within a reasonable time or to release pending trial. Release may be conditioned by guarantees to appear for trial.

4   Everyone who is deprived of his liberty by arrest or detention shall be entitled to take proceedings by which the lawfulness of his detention shall be decided speedily by a court and his release ordered if the detention is not lawful.

5   Everyone who has been the victim of arrest or detention in contravention of the provisions of this Article shall have an enforceable right to compensation.

Changes to legislation: *There are outstanding changes not yet made by the legislation.gov.uk*
editorial team to Human Rights Act 1998. Any changes that have already been made by the team
appear in the content and are referenced with annotations. (See end of Document for details)

ARTICLE 6

RIGHT TO A FAIR TRIAL

1   In the determination of his civil rights and obligations or of any criminal charge against him, everyone is entitled to a fair and public hearing within a reasonable time by an independent and impartial tribunal established by law. Judgment shall be pronounced publicly but the press and public may be excluded from all or part of the trial in the interest of morals, public order or national security in a democratic society, where the interests of juveniles or the protection of the private life of the parties so require, or to the extent strictly necessary in the opinion of the court in special circumstances where publicity would prejudice the interests of justice.

2   Everyone charged with a criminal offence shall be presumed innocent until proved guilty according to law.

3   Everyone charged with a criminal offence has the following minimum rights:
  (a) to be informed promptly, in a language which he understands and in detail, of the nature and cause of the accusation against him;
  (b) to have adequate time and facilities for the preparation of his defence;
  (c) to defend himself in person or through legal assistance of his own choosing or, if he has not sufficient means to pay for legal assistance, to be given it free when the interests of justice so require;
  (d) to examine or have examined witnesses against him and to obtain the attendance and examination of witnesses on his behalf under the same conditions as witnesses against him;
  (e) to have the free assistance of an interpreter if he cannot understand or speak the language used in court.

ARTICLE 7

NO PUNISHMENT WITHOUT LAW

1   No one shall be held guilty of any criminal offence on account of any act or omission which did not constitute a criminal offence under national or international law at the time when it was committed. Nor shall a heavier penalty be imposed than the one that was applicable at the time the criminal offence was committed.

2   This Article shall not prejudice the trial and punishment of any person for any act or omission which, at the time when it was committed, was criminal according to the general principles of law recognised by civilised nations.

ARTICLE 8

RIGHT TO RESPECT FOR PRIVATE AND FAMILY LIFE

1   Everyone has the right to respect for his private and family life, his home and his correspondence.

2   There shall be no interference by a public authority with the exercise of this right except such as is in accordance with the law and is necessary in a democratic society in the interests of national security, public safety or the economic well-being of

the country, for the prevention of disorder or crime, for the protection of health or morals, or for the protection of the rights and freedoms of others.

ARTICLE 9

FREEDOM OF THOUGHT, CONSCIENCE AND RELIGION

1   Everyone has the right to freedom of thought, conscience and religion; this right includes freedom to change his religion or belief and freedom, either alone or in community with others and in public or private, to manifest his religion or belief, in worship, teaching, practice and observance.

2   Freedom to manifest one's religion or beliefs shall be subject only to such limitations as are prescribed by law and are necessary in a democratic society in the interests of public safety, for the protection of public order, health or morals, or for the protection of the rights and freedoms of others.

ARTICLE 10

FREEDOM OF EXPRESSION

1   Everyone has the right to freedom of expression. This right shall include freedom to hold opinions and to receive and impart information and ideas without interference by public authority and regardless of frontiers. This Article shall not prevent States from requiring the licensing of broadcasting, television or cinema enterprises.

2   The exercise of these freedoms, since it carries with it duties and responsibilities, may be subject to such formalities, conditions, restrictions or penalties as are prescribed by law and are necessary in a democratic society, in the interests of national security, territorial integrity or public safety, for the prevention of disorder or crime, for the protection of health or morals, for the protection of the reputation or rights of others, for preventing the disclosure of information received in confidence, or for maintaining the authority and impartiality of the judiciary.

ARTICLE 11

FREEDOM OF ASSEMBLY AND ASSOCIATION

1   Everyone has the right to freedom of peaceful assembly and to freedom of association with others, including the right to form and to join trade unions for the protection of his interests.

2   No restrictions shall be placed on the exercise of these rights other than such as are prescribed by law and are necessary in a democratic society in the interests of national security or public safety, for the prevention of disorder or crime, for the protection of health or morals or for the protection of the rights and freedoms of others. This Article shall not prevent the imposition of lawful restrictions on the exercise of these rights by members of the armed forces, of the police or of the administration of the State.

Changes to legislation: *There are outstanding changes not yet made by the legislation.gov.uk editorial team to Human Rights Act 1998. Any changes that have already been made by the team appear in the content and are referenced with annotations. (See end of Document for details)*

ARTICLE 12

RIGHT TO MARRY

Men and women of marriageable age have the right to marry and to found a family, according to the national laws governing the exercise of this right.

ARTICLE 14

PROHIBITION OF DISCRIMINATION

The enjoyment of the rights and freedoms set forth in this Convention shall be secured without discrimination on any ground such as sex, race, colour, language, religion, political or other opinion, national or social origin, association with a national minority, property, birth or other status.

ARTICLE 16

RESTRICTIONS ON POLITICAL ACTIVITY OF ALIENS

Nothing in Articles 10, 11 and 14 shall be regarded as preventing the High Contracting Parties from imposing restrictions on the political activity of aliens.

ARTICLE 17

PROHIBITION OF ABUSE OF RIGHTS

Nothing in this Convention may be interpreted as implying for any State, group or person any right to engage in any activity or perform any act aimed at the destruction of any of the rights and freedoms set forth herein or at their limitation to a greater extent than is provided for in the Convention.

ARTICLE 18

LIMITATION ON USE OF RESTRICTIONS ON RIGHTS

The restrictions permitted under this Convention to the said rights and freedoms shall not be applied for any purpose other than those for which they have been prescribed.

Changes to legislation: There are outstanding changes not yet made by the legislation.gov.uk
editorial team to Human Rights Act 1998. Any changes that have already been made by the team
appear in the content and are referenced with annotations. (See end of Document for details)

PART II

THE FIRST PROTOCOL

ARTICLE 1

PROTECTION OF PROPERTY

Every natural or legal person is entitled to the peaceful enjoyment of his possessions. No one shall be deprived of his possessions except in the public interest and subject to the conditions provided for by law and by the general principles of international law.

The preceding provisions shall not, however, in any way impair the right of a State to enforce such laws as it deems necessary to control the use of property in accordance with the general interest or to secure the payment of taxes or other contributions or penalties.

ARTICLE 2

RIGHT TO EDUCATION

No person shall be denied the right to education. In the exercise of any functions which it assumes in relation to education and to teaching, the State shall respect the right of parents to ensure such education and teaching in conformity with their own religious and philosophical convictions.

ARTICLE 3

RIGHT TO FREE ELECTIONS

The High Contracting Parties undertake to hold free elections at reasonable intervals by secret ballot, under conditions which will ensure the free expression of the opinion of the people in the choice of the legislature.

[*F44*PART 3

ARTICLE 1 OF THE THIRTEENTH PROTOCOL

ABOLITION OF THE DEATH PENALTY

Annotations:

Amendments (Textual)
F44 Sch. 1 Pt. 3 substituted (22.6.2004) by The Human Rights Act 1998 (Amendment) Order 2004 (S.I. 2004/1574), **art. 2(3)**

The death penalty shall be abolished. No one shall be condemned to such penalty or executed.]

Changes to legislation: There are outstanding changes not yet made by the legislation.gov.uk editorial team to Human Rights Act 1998. Any changes that have already been made by the team appear in the content and are referenced with annotations. (See end of Document for details)

PART III

THE SIXTH PROTOCOL

. . . .

SCHEDULE 2   Section 10.

REMEDIAL ORDERS

Orders

1   (1) A remedial order may—

   (a)   contain such incidental, supplemental, consequential or transitional provision as the person making it considers appropriate;

   (b)   be made so as to have effect from a date earlier than that on which it is made;

   (c)   make provision for the delegation of specific functions;

   (d)   make different provision for different cases.

   (2) The power conferred by sub-paragraph (1)(a) includes—

   (a)   power to amend primary legislation (including primary legislation other than that which contains the incompatible provision); and

   (b)   power to amend or revoke subordinate legislation (including subordinate legislation other than that which contains the incompatible provision).

   (3) A remedial order may be made so as to have the same extent as the legislation which it affects.

   (4) No person is to be guilty of an offence solely as a result of the retrospective effect of a remedial order.

Procedure

2   No remedial order may be made unless—

   (a)   a draft of the order has been approved by a resolution of each House of Parliament made after the end of the period of 60 days beginning with the day on which the draft was laid; or

   (b)   it is declared in the order that it appears to the person making it that, because of the urgency of the matter, it is necessary to make the order without a draft being so approved.

Orders laid in draft

3   (1) No draft may be laid under paragraph 2(a) unless—

   (a)   the person proposing to make the order has laid before Parliament a document which contains a draft of the proposed order and the required information; and

   (b)   the period of 60 days, beginning with the day on which the document required by this sub-paragraph was laid, has ended.

Changes to legislation: There are outstanding changes not yet made by the legislation.gov.uk editorial team to Human Rights Act 1998. Any changes that have already been made by the team appear in the content and are referenced with annotations. (See end of Document for details)

(2) If representations have been made during that period, the draft laid under paragraph 2(a) must be accompanied by a statement containing—

    (a)   a summary of the representations; and

    (b)   if, as a result of the representations, the proposed order has been changed, details of the changes.

Urgent cases

4   (1) If a remedial order ("the original order") is made without being approved in draft, the person making it must lay it before Parliament, accompanied by the required information, after it is made.

(2) If representations have been made during the period of 60 days beginning with the day on which the original order was made, the person making it must (after the end of that period) lay before Parliament a statement containing—

    (a)   a summary of the representations; and

    (b)   if, as a result of the representations, he considers it appropriate to make changes to the original order, details of the changes.

(3) If sub-paragraph (2)(b) applies, the person making the statement must—

    (a)   make a further remedial order replacing the original order; and

    (b)   lay the replacement order before Parliament.

(4) If, at the end of the period of 120 days beginning with the day on which the original order was made, a resolution has not been passed by each House approving the original or replacement order, the order ceases to have effect (but without that affecting anything previously done under either order or the power to make a fresh remedial order).

Definitions

5   In this Schedule—

    "representations" means representations about a remedial order (or proposed remedial order) made to the person making (or proposing to make) it and includes any relevant Parliamentary report or resolution; and

    "required information" means—

    (a)   an explanation of the incompatibility which the order (or proposed order) seeks to remove, including particulars of the relevant declaration, finding or order; and

    (b)   a statement of the reasons for proceeding under section 10 and for making an order in those terms.

Calculating periods

6   In calculating any period for the purposes of this Schedule, no account is to be taken of any time during which—

    (a)   Parliament is dissolved or prorogued; or

    (b)   both Houses are adjourned for more than four days.

[F48 7   (1) This paragraph applies in relation to–

Changes to legislation: There are outstanding changes not yet made by the legislation.gov.uk editorial team to Human Rights Act 1998. Any changes that have already been made by the team appear in the content and are referenced with annotations. (See end of Document for details)

(a) any remedial order made, and any draft of such an order proposed to be made,–

    (i) by the Scottish Ministers; or

    (ii) within devolved competence (within the meaning of the Scotland Act 1998) by Her Majesty in Council; and

(b) any document or statement to be laid in connection with such an order (or proposed order).

(2) This Schedule has effect in relation to any such order (or proposed order), document or statement subject to the following modifications.

(3) Any reference to Parliament, each House of Parliament or both Houses of Parliament shall be construed as a reference to the Scottish Parliament.

(4) Paragraph 6 does not apply and instead, in calculating any period for the purposes of this Schedule, no account is to be taken of any time during which the Scottish Parliament is dissolved or is in recess for more than four days.]

Annotations:

Amendments (Textual)

F48 Sch. 2 para. 7 inserted (27.7.2000) by S.I. 2000/2040, art 2, **Sch. Pt. I para. 21** (with art. 3)

SCHEDULE 3

Sections 14 and 15.

DEROGATION AND RESERVATION

F49

PART I

. . . .

Annotations:

Amendments (Textual)

F49 Sch. 3 Pt. I repealed (1.4.2001) by S.I. 2001/1216, **art. 4**

F50

PART I

DEROGATION

. . . .

Changes to legislation: There are outstanding changes not yet made by the legislation.gov.uk editorial team to Human Rights Act 1998. Any changes that have already been made by the team appear in the content and are referenced with annotations. (See end of Document for details)

Annotations:

Amendments (Textual)

F50 Sch. 3 Pt. I repealed (8.4.2005) by The Human Rights Act 1998 (Amendment) Order 2005 (S.I. 2005/1071), **art. 2**

PART II

RESERVATION

At the time of signing the present (First) Protocol, I declare that, in view of certain provisions of the Education Acts in the United Kingdom, the principle affirmed in the second sentence of Article 2 is accepted by the United Kingdom only so far as it is compatible with the provision of efficient instruction and training, and the avoidance of unreasonable public expenditure.

Dated 20 March 1952

Made by the United Kingdom Permanent Representative to the Council of Europe.

SCHEDULE 4   Section 18(6).

JUDICIAL PENSIONS

Duty to make orders about pensions

1   (1) The appropriate Minister must by order make provision with respect to pensions payable to or in respect of any holder of a judicial office who serves as an ECHR judge.

(2) A pensions order must include such provision as the Minister making it considers is necessary to secure that—

(a)   an ECHR judge who was, immediately before his appointment as an ECHR judge, a member of a judicial pension scheme is entitled to remain as a member of that scheme;

(b)   the terms on which he remains a member of the scheme are those which would have been applicable had he not been appointed as an ECHR judge; and

(c)   entitlement to benefits payable in accordance with the scheme continues to be determined as if, while serving as an ECHR judge, his salary was that which would (but for section 18(4)) have been payable to him in respect of his continuing service as the holder of his judicial office.

Contributions

2   A pensions order may, in particular, make provision—

(a)   for any contributions which are payable by a person who remains a member of a scheme as a result of the order, and which would otherwise be payable by deduction from his salary, to be made otherwise than by deduction from his salary as an ECHR judge; and

Changes to legislation: There are outstanding changes not yet made by the legislation.gov.uk editorial team to Human Rights Act 1998. Any changes that have already been made by the team appear in the content and are referenced with annotations. (See end of Document for details)

(b) for such contributions to be collected in such manner as may be determined by the administrators of the scheme.

Amendments of other enactments

3   A pensions order may amend any provision of, or made under, a pensions Act in such manner and to such extent as the Minister making the order considers necessary or expedient to ensure the proper administration of any scheme to which it relates.

Definitions

4   In this Schedule—

"appropriate Minister" means—

(a) in relation to any judicial office whose jurisdiction is exercisable exclusively in relation to Scotland, the Secretary of State; and

(b) otherwise, the Lord Chancellor;

"ECHR judge" means the holder of a judicial office who is serving as a judge of the Court;

"judicial pension scheme" means a scheme established by and in accordance with a pensions Act;

"pensions Act" means—

(a) the [M17]County Courts Act Northern Ireland) 1959;

(b) the [M18]Sheriffs' Pensions (Scotland) Act 1961;

(c) the [M19]Judicial Pensions Act 1981; or

(d) the [M20]Judicial Pensions and Retirement Act 1993; and

"pensions order" means an order made under paragraph 1.

Annotations:

Marginal Citations

M17   1959 c. 25 (N.I.).

M18   1961 c. 42.

M19   1981 c. 20.

M20   1993 c. 8.

Changes to legislation:
There are outstanding changes not yet made by the legislation.gov.uk editorial team to Human Rights Act 1998. Any changes that have already been made by the team appear in the content and are referenced with annotations.

Changes and effects yet to be applied to :
–   s. 4(5)(f) words substituted by 2013 c. 22 Sch. 14 para. 5(5)
–   Sch. 4 para. 4 words inserted by 2013 c. 25 Sch. 8 para. 26

Commencement Orders yet to be applied to the Human Rights Act 1998
Commencement Orders bringing legislation that affects this Act into force:
–   S.I. 2006/1014 art. 2 Sch. 1 2 commences (2005 c. 4)
–   S.I. 2007/1897 art. 2 commences (2005 c. 9)
–   S.I. 2009/812 art. 3(a)(b) commences (2006 c. 52)
–   S.I. 2009/1059 Order transitional provisions for effects of commencing SI 2009/812
–   S.I. 2009/1604 art. 2 commences (2005 c. 4)

Acknowledgements

I owe so much to my mother for reading to me and my father for arguing with me. I am grateful to a lifetime of wonderful teachers, mentors and friends – whether mentioned or not in my human rights story; you know who you are. James Sebastian, Jane, Stella, Tamara, Fi Mac, Diana, the Butters (especially my goddaughter Emilia), the II-As, Clare, Jude and Andrew, Anthony, Amrit, Cathy, Julie, Kevin, Domino, Sandi, DJ, Janet, Magda, Linda, Will G, Shyama, Vivienne, Tizer, Nicola B, Fiona S, Emilie H, B and best friend Fi H. You know why.

Thanks to Tom Penn at Penguin, who asked me to write *On Liberty*, and to Richard Duguid, Kate Watson, Ingrid Matts and Jim Stoddart for making the publishing process such a pleasure. Freelance copy-editor Bela Cunha brought years of experience to this challenge, with so much kindness and humility. Thank you. Thanks to Sam Johnson for organizing my bizarre blind photoshoot, to Paul Stuart for the covershot, and make-up maestro Lindsey Poole for my cheekbones and confidence. Jo Metson Scott took the author picture complete with eyes.

It's hard to articulate sufficient gratitude to my dear friends Rachel Holmes (a distinguished 'Writer at Liberty') and Mairi Clare Rodgers (Liberty's Media Director) for reading the full manuscript with such meticulous care and skill. And to all my extraordinary Liberty colleagues – named and yet to be named in our vital continuing struggle – especially Ian McDonald, Jess Kaplan, Penny Morrow and George Pope. Frances Butler is our wise Chair and the late great Christine Jackson and Sue Baring have been rocks as successive Chairs of the Civil Liberties Trust. Liberty members past, present and future. You make it happen.

This book is for you, Bean. You and your generation are the point of and hope for everything.

Index